JOHNSON INSTITUTE®
Minneapolis

Parenting for Prevention

How to Raise a Child to Say No to Alcohol and Other Drugs

For Parents, Teachers, and Other Concerned Adults

Revised Edition

David J. Wilmes

Edited by Cyril A. Reilly

JOHNSON INSTITUTE®
Minneapolis

Johnson Institute-QVS, Inc.

7205 Ohms Lane

Minneapolis, Minnesota 55439-2159

612/831-1630 or 800/231-5165

Library of Congress Cataloging-in-Publication Data

Wilmes, David J.
    Parenting for prevention, How to raise a child to say no to alcohol and other drugs: for parents, teachers, and other concerned adults / David J. Wilmes: edited by Cyril A. Reilly. — Rev. ed.

        p.   cm.
    Includes bibliographical references (p.   ) and index.
    ISBN 0-935908-46-3
    1. Children—United States—Drug use. 2. Children—United States—Alcohol use. 3. Drug abuse—United States—Prevention. 4. Alcoholism—United States—Prevention. 5. Parenting—United States.   I. Reilly, Cyril A., 1920-   II. Title.
    HV5824.C45W55 1995
    649'.4—dc20   95-5904
                                                               CIP

Printed in the United States of America
99 98   / 6 5 4 3 2

As the first edition of *Parenting for Prevention* was coming off the press, my mom died as a result of complications related to Parkinson's disease. This book is dedicated to her and my dad.

Acknowledgments

The ideas in *Parenting for Prevention* are really the result of a number of incredible people with whom I've had the opportunity to work. I would like to mention a few:

- Mr. Carl D. Miller and the Miller Family Foundation, who have been an ongoing inspiration. Mr. Miller's personal commitment to the vital issue of parent education has made it possible for hundreds of thousands of parents to get critical parenting information that will make a difference in their children's future.

- The students and staff who have participated in the Johnson Institute *StudentView*® Survey. Their participation has made a significant contribution to the field of prevention. Thanks to: Bud Remboldt, the visionary behind the instrument; Dee Stuart, who insisted that the data be user-friendly; and Dr. Patricia Harrison and Dr. Michael Luxenberg, who insure the validity and reliability of the data.

- All of the staff at the Johnson Institute. Your daily hard work and willingness to "get the job done" is a constant source of support and inspiration.

- Pat Stevens, Sue Stevens, Mary Kay Wood, Carol Christy, Dave Zarek, Steve Nelson and all of the staff, clients, and their families with whom I had the privilege to work at New Connection Programs from 1971 to 1984.

- Carole Remboldt and Cy Reilly for their persistence and patience in helping me focus on the tedious task of writing.

- Most importantly, thanks to my partner and parenting confidante, Connie. Our marriage continues to be my source of joy and fulfillment. Thanks to Scott and Michael for being the best kids any parent could hope for.

Contents

Introduction

You should know two things right away about this book: what it does and doesn't deal with, and how it can help you and your family.

First, this book is about preventing kids from using alcohol and other drugs.* As a parent and a professional counselor living in today's turbulent world, I dream about raising a family in which no child of mine will ever start using alcohol or other drugs. I dream of raising my family in such a way as to prevent the agony that comes when alcohol or other drugs invade our family circle. Using the knowledge I've gained over the years, I've written this book to help you make such a

---

*You'll notice I use the phrase "alcohol and other drugs" throughout this book. I do so to **emphasize** that alcohol is a drug—just like cocaine, marijuana, uppers, downers, or any other mind-altering substance. Too often people talk about "alcohol **or** drugs" or alcohol **and** drugs" as if alcohol were somehow different from drugs and in a category by itself. True, our culture, our government, even our laws treat alcohol differently from the way they treat other drugs such as pot, crack, or heroin. But the symptoms of addiction are essentially the same for all the mind-altering substances, and the need to find ways to prevent their use is just as urgent. Also, I sometimes use the term "chemical dependence" because it covers addiction to all these mind-altering substances and because it's short and simple.

dream come true for yourselves. (If your kids are already seriously into chemicals, the book you should by all means start with is Dick Schaefer's *Choices & Consequences: What to Do When a Teenager Uses Alcohol/Drugs*—published by the Johnson Institute.)

Second, *Parenting for Prevention* can be immensely valuable to you because of two unusual features. For one, it's addressed directly to parents. You might be surprised that that's unusual, but it is. For, strangely enough, authors who write about kids' problems with alcohol and other drugs often talk to educators, or other professionals, not to parents. I'm convinced that that's a mistake. On the basis of my own experience both as a parent and as a professional who's dealt with hundreds of kids and their families during the last twenty years, I'm convinced that **parents** are the ones who not only can but must take the lead in preventing their kids from getting mixed up with alcohol and other drugs.

The second unusual feature of this book is that it takes a positive, constructive, wide-ranging approach to prevention by showing parents how to teach **life skills** to their kids. It avoids negative approaches such as using scare tactics on kids; it avoids partial approaches such as teaching self-esteem as if it were a cure-all (self-esteem is valuable, even indispensable, but it simply isn't enough.)

What are these life skills, and why are they so important in preventing alcohol and other drug problems in our kids? Part 2 will explain at length. For now, I'll mention only the highlights.

Life skills are a whole set of **social skills**—skills that enable us to be at ease in our many and varied contacts with other persons. They're an assortment of positive feelings, beliefs, and behaviors that help us handle stress and be healthy psychologically as well as physically. We're talking about such basic skills as being confident and self-reliant and being able to communicate effectively with others (to mention only a few). These life skills build energy rather than drain it; they heal our wounds and strengthen us for living happily and productively, both as individuals and as members of a group. People who have these skills set goals and reach them; they manage their time well; they build a supportive network of family and friends; they take responsibility for their feelings, thoughts, and actions. (Incidentally, one of the great benefits of using this book is that as you follow its suggestions for helping your kids to develop these basic life skills, you too are challenged to reexamine your own feelings, beliefs, and behavior. So it gives you a real opportunity to look inward and to sharpen your own life skills.

But what do life skills have to do with preventing alcohol and other drug problems in our kids? **Everything.** They're the best preventive medicine there is. Why? Because they're a long-range, common sense, well-tested set of skills that develop well-balanced kids in a healthy family setting. They're **not** a quick fix, not a magic formula, not a one-minute-a-day program that promises effortless, painless solutions to the complex problems of parenting in an alcohol and other drug-oriented culture. Rather, they're comparable to a long-range physical wellness program where day after day, year after year, you faithfully cling to a positive program of sound nutrition, exercise, sleep, recreation, and relaxation that slowly builds a sound body—the best **prevention** program ever.

I make you a promise. If you read this book thoughtfully and follow its recommendations, you'll gain **new insights** into a whole host of everyday parenting problems as well as **practical skills** for handling them. Those insights and skills will be the best insurance policy you can take out to prevent your kids from getting into problems with alcohol or other drugs—because you'll be helping them develop into well-balanced kids who can stand on their own two feet, resist undue peer pressures, and still be accepted and respected wherever they go.

PART 1

Foundations for Teaching Life Skills

1

Parents as Enablers:
Hurting the Ones We Love

This book is about ways to prevent your kids from ever getting hooked on alcohol or other drugs. In Part 2 we'll discuss your part in helping kids develop life skills that will prevent them from having alcohol or other drug problems. In this chapter we'll begin to clear the way for that program by discussing how to **avoid or get rid** of things that might harm your kids later on—something like keeping the weeds from ever getting started in your garden, or at least getting rid of them early, before they take over.

The Meaning of Enabling

It's only fair to warn you that some poisonous weeds might already be sprouting in your garden. And these weeds are doubly dangerous because they're the kind we usually don't even see. Professionals in the field of chemical dependence have a name for them that at first confuses laypersons: **enabling.** To begin understanding the concept of enabling, read the following statements about yourself and then indicate with a yes or no whether you agree or disagree. (Later on in the chapter we'll have a more extensive checklist.)

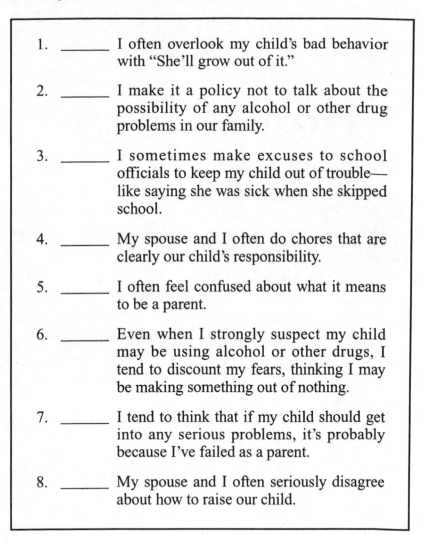

1. _____ I often overlook my child's bad behavior with "She'll grow out of it."

2. _____ I make it a policy not to talk about the possibility of any alcohol or other drug problems in our family.

3. _____ I sometimes make excuses to school officials to keep my child out of trouble— like saying she was sick when she skipped school.

4. _____ My spouse and I often do chores that are clearly our child's responsibility.

5. _____ I often feel confused about what it means to be a parent.

6. _____ Even when I strongly suspect my child may be using alcohol or other drugs, I tend to discount my fears, thinking I may be making something out of nothing.

7. _____ I tend to think that if my child should get into any serious problems, it's probably because I've failed as a parent.

8. _____ My spouse and I often seriously disagree about how to raise our child.

If you're like most parents, you probably answered yes to at least some of those statements. You've probably done those things for what seem like good reasons: to keep your kids from being unhappy, to give them the benefit of the doubt, to keep peace in the family. Unfortunately, though, despite your good intentions you might have been doing exactly the opposite. The experts call it enabling.

Usually "enabling" has a positive meaning: encouraging or supporting someone or something. But here it's negative, because we're talking about encouraging or supporting something that's destructive. In the context of this book, here's what enabling means:

Enabling is a process whereby well-meaning parents unwittingly allow and even encourage irresponsible and self-destructive behavior in their children by shielding them from the consequences of their actions.

Since this book is about parenting that will help us **prevent** our kids from getting into trouble with alcohol or other drugs, we're saying that enabling is an ineffective kind of parenting that does just the opposite: it actually paves the way for kids to make wrong choices about alcohol and drugs. (Or, to use our earlier image, we're actually **watering** the weeds in the garden!)

To illustrate what enabling is, let's look at Steve and his son Tim, a promising tenth-grade hockey player. Tim had some behavior problems in grade school, but his involvement in hockey seemed to settle him down somewhat. Lately, however, he's been acting defiant again. Early in the year the coach explained the state athletic code that forbids any use of alcohol or other drugs, and of course Tim promised to observe it. But a few weeks later, Steve, out for a walk, came upon Tim and some buddies drinking beer in a parked car. Steve was angry, but Tim made up a story: When his buddies asked him to go for a ride, he had no idea they had beer in the car. He refused and refused to join them in a few beers but finally, under pressure, gave in. But it was the first time he'd ever had a beer—honest. The real story was that Tim and his buddies had been drinking beer together the last several months. They'd either slip a few cans out of the house or they'd get an older friend to buy it at a liquor store.

Skeptical at first, Steve finally swallowed the whole story, thought it over, and decided to say nothing to the coach or anyone else about it. After all, what if Tim should get kicked off the team? And what if one little incident like that could even end up wrecking a possibly brilliant career in professional hockey (a career Steve had often dreamed of for himself, by the way)? No need to tell Mom either; she'd just make a big deal of it and worry herself to death. In the long run, too, the little secret favor would make Tim think more highly of him (they'd had a few spats lately). No, just forget the whole thing.

What has happened is pretty clear. By protecting Tim from the consequences of his unwise choice to drink beer contrary to his promise, Steve has enabled him (encouraged him) to make future irresponsible choices. "After all," we can hear Tim say, "nothing happened, did it?" Notice, too, that Steve's silence has weakened family ties. Keeping Mom in the dark has prevented her from sharing her insights into the problem. Finally, it's been a rather cheap (but ultimately costly) way for Steve to get on the good side of an adolescent who's been hard to handle lately.

How to Detect Enabling

The many implications of the Steve/Tim story indicate that enabling is quite a complex process. And a seemingly small incident like this could be just one of many dozens that occur in a typical family and somehow intertwine to create a whole environment of enabling. The incident illustrates a second point: It's hard to detect enabling in oneself. If someone accused Steve of poor judgment and even of some unconsciously self-serving motives, he'd probably flatly deny them—and in good faith.

If enabling is so complex and hard to detect, how can we find out if we've let it become a part of our own parenting? By examining three basic aspects of our personalities that color our whole approach to life: our feelings, beliefs, and behaviors. The way we handle these three will largely determine the character of our family life.

How Our Feelings Can Contribute to Enabling

As parents we of course love our children, so our feelings are deeply engaged wherever they're concerned. Those deep, intense feelings we have for them are a wonderful source of joy and power, as any parent knows. Memories of times spent with our kids bring us some of our happiest experiences; emotion-laden love for them can make our daily sacrifices for them easy and perhaps even call forth such heroism that we'd willingly die for a beloved child. But if we divorce our feelings from solid values and sound judgment, if we don't examine our feelings or don't express them well in our words or behavior, or if our kids misinterpret them, our feelings can easily contribute to enabling. To show what I mean, let's look at some examples of how our feelings can help to make us enablers if we don't handle them well.

The Protective Instinct

As parents we naturally want to protect our kids from danger. But the instinct can easily go astray. When Jill was put on detention for allegedly writing obscenities on a classroom chalkboard, she told her dad she hadn't done it (actually she had). Her dad stormed over to the school, created a scene in the principal's office, and threatened to take Jill out of school if she didn't get "fair treatment." Why did he act that way? Fearful that his daughter was being mistreated, he angrily overreacted and attempted to "rescue" her without really knowing what had happened. Such "rescue" attempts, prompted by unresolved fear and anger, foster irresponsibility in kids. This is a clear case of enabling behavior.

Self-doubt

Mary, a recently divorced mother, didn't know what to say when son Jack kept begging for permission to go to a party. She didn't know who would be there or what would be going on, but she finally gave in. Why? Not because she felt the party was something he should go to but because ever since her divorce she's felt guilty and insecure and hasn't been able to take a firm stand on anything. Self-doubts often make for unsound judgments. Naturally, our children suffer from our insecurity, either because they shrewdly take advantage of it to talk us into unwise decisions like Mary's, or because our very indecisiveness makes them feel insecure about making decisions. In either case, the way we handle our feelings of self-doubt can be an enabling factor because our children are learning to make unwise choices—as they might well do soon in regard to using alcohol or other drugs.

Fear

Terri first ran away from home when she was 10. Now, whenever she doesn't get her way she threatens to leave. Her parents have tried to hold her accountable, but the threat of her leaving home and not coming back or of being injured or kidnapped has immobilized them with fear. They've found it easier just to give in. Neither parent wants to bear the responsibility for something terrible that might happen to her if she should run away again. Their fear is enabling Terri to get her way whether it's good for her or not; her parents are enabling her to learn irresponsibility.

Performance Anxiety

These days we often hear how kids suffer from "performance anxiety": "Mom and Dad will **kill** me if I don't get all A's." "What if I fall flat on my face in the figure-skating competition?" "What if I dress all wrong for the party?"

We often feel similar anxiety.

- "I've got to be a perfect parent so I can prove that a single parent can do a good job."

- "I've got to see to it that Dave cleans up his messy room; if he doesn't, I will."

- "I've got to be sure Sheila hears the alarm and gets to school on time."

- "I've got to make sure Sarah practices her flute more—I want her to be first chair before the spring concert."

- "I hope I don't embarrass them by saying something stupid when they bring their friends home."

What all this amounts to is unrealistic expectations that make us feel anxious, place impossible demands on us, drain our energies, and make us hard to live with. When we internalize this level of anxiety about our children's performance, we run the risk of enabling by becoming overly responsible for their achievement or lack of achievement.

Anger

There are plenty of anger-producing incidents in the average home: Bobby using Dad's new saw to cut a steel bolt, Melissa tracking across the white carpet with muddy shoes, endless bickering over who gets the window seat on the trip to Grandma's. Some parents overreact: screaming obscenities, calling the kids names, making wild threats. The result? Kids learn to turn off **all** parental reactions they dislike, including those concerning alcohol and other drugs. Other parents underreact, convinced they should avoid conflict at any cost. The underreacting parent really wages a cold war based on grim silence—and creates a tense home where everyone walks on eggshells. Pent-up feelings can strongly tempt kids to turn to alcohol or other drugs.

How Our Beliefs Can Contribute to Enabling

Our beliefs come from a wide variety of sources: experience, family, teachers, religion, neighbors, TV, books, magazines, newspapers. Without beliefs we're rudderless ships. But beliefs vary immensely in value: from rock solid ones grounded firmly in experience and common sense to oversimplified ones based on sexual stereotypes ("Real men never cry.") or superstitious folklore ("Never let a black cat cross your path.") to the superficial slogans of bumper stickers ("Truckers make better lovers.") and TV commercials ("Weekends were made for Michelob.").

Parenting too has its mistaken beliefs that can take us further along the slippery path called enabling. Here are a few such beliefs—and how they can contribute to our enabling.

Mistaken Belief #1

"I can't expect my child to be responsible for herself; there are just too many pressures on kids today."

True, there are heavier-than-ever pressures on kids today: peer pressures, pressures from the media (movies, videocassettes, rock stars and their lyrics, slick TV and magazine ads, to name a few), and many other kinds. But heavy pressures still don't excuse irresponsible behavior; all of us, young or old, have to answer for our decisions. So when Alex's father dismisses repeated reports of unexcused absences with "Kids that age always get into some trouble" or with "It's his friend Andy who always talks him into it," he's clearly looking for excuses instead of reasons. That's enabling.

Mistaken Belief #2

"There's nothing I can do. I'm the last person my kids listen to."

All of us have thought that way, I'm sure—especially if our kids are in early adolescence (10-13), when kids actually seem to gloat over their ability to ignore anything we say. But reliable research shows exactly the opposite: One of the key factors that kids consider when they choose whether or not to use alcohol or other drugs is what they think their parents' reaction will be. We can and we must actively shape our kids' decisions, particularly by helping them develop life skills (as we'll see in Part 2). To give up on that responsibility clearly encourages our kids to make ill-considered, irresponsible choices.

Mistaken Belief #3

"If everybody else is doing it, it must be okay."

Most of us would deny believing this—it seems so absurd when we examine it rationally. In practice, though, it's often the real reason we allow kids to do things we think aren't good for them ("After all, the Thompsons are good parents, and they think it's all right—and the Murdochs and the Blaines and the Bradfords and the Schmidts, too. I must be the one who's off base.") When Susan was in third grade "everybody" in her class had pierced ears, wore designer jeans, and used makeup and perfume, so her parents let her do it. In sixth grade, "everybody" went to slumber parties where they showed R-rated movies. In ninth grade "everybody" was going to parties where they served alcohol, and it was too late to say no.

What's the answer to "everybody's doing it"? We have to decide early what our values and norms and limits are. Our kids need (and actually want, contrary to what we often hear) clear, firm, consistent guidelines. Giving in to "everybody's doing it" sets us up to enable any number of self-destructive patterns of behavior in our kids.

Mistaken Belief #4

"If I love my kids, I must always trust them."

Not so. Love and trust are two different things. Love is unconditional: Nothing my kids could ever do would make me stop loving them. Trust is another story. As kids grow up and begin to test our limits by pushing beyond the agreed-upon guidelines, it's only natural that our trust is shaken.

So when kids grind away at us with the dull, rusty cliché, "If you loved me, you'd trust me. So why can't I stay out till midnight?," we should see that they're really asking us to be enablers who will help them make poor choices. So we can answer, "I couldn't possibly love you more than I do, but at this point you've earned enough trust to be out till 10 o'clock. When you prove you can handle that amount of free time, we'll see about more of it."

How Our Behavior Can Contribute to Enabling

The way we handle our feelings and beliefs, as we've just seen, can move us toward enabling: toward influencing our kids in ways that impel them toward self-destructive choices. However, since feelings and beliefs are basically internal, they're not necessarily displayed outwardly. But our behaviors are by their very nature external: Kids can see them, even sometimes literally feel them with their bodies (as when we hug them, for instance). So behaviors of the **wrong** kind can be even more powerful enablers than our feelings or beliefs. Here are a few typical enabling behaviors.

Keeping Secrets

Secrets can be wholesome fun: a surprise birthday party, a gift slyly slipped into the house, an unexpected vacation you've quietly set up for the family. But other secrets can be the beginning of serious problems with enabling.

Remember how Steve kept it a secret both from the coach and from his wife when he discovered his son and his son's friends drinking beer in the car? Such secrets can erect barriers and create hidden alliances that make open communication impossible. As we protect our kids from the normal consequences of their acts by keeping the wrong kind of secrets, we establish ourselves as enablers. And small secrets open the floodgates to more and bigger secrets.

Giving in to Avoid Conflict

Most of us dislike conflict, and it often seems easier to give in than to be firm and have to face the seemingly inevitable arguments, whining, pouting, or tantrums that follow. Susan, who's had a bad day at the office, picks up son Jeremy at school, where he's had a bad day too. He's alternately loud and surly on the way home. At home he doesn't want any dinner but wants to visit at Randy's house instead. So Susan gives in—it just isn't worth the hassle.

What Susan has actually done is teach Jeremy that if he raises enough fuss he'll get his way. Jeremy is on his way to developing serious problems, thanks to Susan's enabling behavior.

Shielding Kids from Consequences

When Ellen was caught smoking cigarettes in the restroom at school, she was suspended from the basketball team for two weeks. Her father was enraged: Should a little infraction interrupt her basketball career? So he contacted an old friend who was on the school board, and Ellen was quietly reinstated on the team.

Interfering with the natural consequences of a kid's conduct delivers powerful messages: "You're above the rules" and "Daddy will always be there to bail you out." It's a particularly destructive form of enabling, and it often backfires in unexpected ways. Daddy has always bailed Ellen out of her difficulties, so they've always been the best of buddies. But later when she was in college and he failed to find her an attorney who was able to get her driver's license reinstated after her second DWI, she turned against him and hasn't spoken to him since. After all, Daddy had finally showed he didn't really love her, hadn't he?

Doing Kids' Work for Them

Kevin's daily chore is the immensely time-consuming, exhausting, humiliating task of taking out the garbage. So he often "forgets" it. Since his mother can't stand the sight of messy, overflowing wastebaskets, she takes it out for him. In the long run, she figures, it's easier to do it herself.

This is a good example of enabling that begins in small, harmless things. Actually, taking out the garbage is Kevin's only tangible contribution to the family. When his mother takes on his responsibility, she's sending him at least three wrong messages: Your contribution isn't really important; others will do your work for you; and (to interpret it as a wide-ranging rule for life) irresponsible behavior has no undesirable consequences. Enabling at its worst!

Summary

As I've worked these last twenty years with hundreds of families suffering the pain of kids' addictions, I've found that parental enabling patterns usually begin long before the young person ever uses alcohol or other drugs. If we **understand** what enabling is, **identify** our own enabling feelings, beliefs, and behaviors at their earliest stages, unflinchingly **admit** what we've been doing, and then courageously **stop** those patterns, we'll be well on our way to preventing our kids from falling into destructive patterns that can easily lead them to alcohol or other drug problems and possible addiction.

The positive alternative to enabling is, as we've mentioned, the building of life skills. But before we go into that, you need to arm yourself with solid, basic information about alcohol and other drugs. That's what Chapter 2 will give you.

2

Facts About Kids' Use of Alcohol and Other Drugs

Whether you and I like it or not, alcohol and other drugs are a fact of life in today's world—and especially in our kids' world. Sooner or later, in one way or another, our kids are going to have to make choices about alcohol and other drugs, as surely as they have to make choices about studies, friendships, sex, athletics, clothes, cars, a career.

If we expect to be helpful when our kids face tough choices in any area, they of course have to know we're available. But they also need to have confidence that—to put it bluntly—we know what we're talking about. In few areas arc they so likely to be disappointed in us as in our knowledge about alcohol and other drugs. Many of us are proud that we've never even touched drugs—at least nonalcoholic ones. Good. But use (or abuse) is one thing; lack of knowledge—or worse, erroneous "knowledge"—is quite another.

If we really don't know the basics about alcohol or other drugs and how today's kids relate to them, our kids see right through us. Today's kids are smart. Even if they've never touched alcohol and other drugs themselves, they know—or soon will know—friends and classmates who are into them up to their ears; and many of them have read about alcohol and other drugs, discussed them in class, heard lectures by experts.

So if we try to discuss alcohol and other drugs by dragging in a few pious clichés, or if we come up with attitudes or "facts" that reveal ignorance or misinformation or prejudice, they'll turn us right off.

In short, when it comes time to discuss alcohol and other drugs, what our kids need and want from us, besides a love that bespeaks openness and concern and availability, is accurate, up-to-date, relevant knowledge—knowledge that tells them "Mom and Dad are really with it. They understand alcohol and other drugs, and they understand our problems with them." So in this chapter we'll discuss in an objective way some basic truths about alcohol and other drugs in relation to our kids: why kids use them; which ones they use; where, when (at what age), and how they use them. If alcohol and other drugs are one of our wiliest and strongest enemies— as they are—we'd better know about them before we try to battle them.

Why Kids Use Alcohol and Other Drugs

As we search for ways to prevent our kids from getting involved with alcohol and other drugs, we inevitably wonder why they'd ever want to use them in the first place. When kids do get involved, the question often takes the form of "Who's to blame?"

What Parents Say About Why

We tend to look for the culprit, perhaps unconsciously seeking to transfer any responsibility to others. Typical answers parents give as to why kids use alcohol and other drugs tend to blame:

- **The school:** "Can't those teachers see what's going on? Don't the kids get any supervision at all?"

- **Other parents:** "Well, what can you expect from a home like that?"

- **The peer group:** "Jamie never had any problems till he got in with that bunch."

- **Pushers or bar owners:** "Put the pushers in jail and close up those sleazy places, and we'd have this thing licked."

- **The media:** "What can you expect when the movies take it for granted that it's cool to use drugs?"

- **The police:** "If the cops were on the ball they'd pick up those kids the first time they got out of line and that'd be the end of it." Or: "If the cops wouldn't hound the kids as if they were all criminals, they wouldn't even think of using drugs. You get what you expect."

- **Role models:** "Those rock stars are all into drugs just like the professional athletes. And these are the ones our kids want to be like!"

What Kids Say About Why

But when we ask the kids themselves why they get into alcohol or other drugs, we get a very different set of answers.

- "I wanted to see how I'd feel."
- "I just wanted to have some fun."
- "I like to take risks."
- "I'm no baby. I can make up my own mind."
- "I like to experiment with new things."
- "I wanted to feel grown up."
- "I wanted to be part of the group."
- "I didn't want to be a nerd."

Analysis of Contrasting Answers

Looking at the contrasting (not to say contradictory) answers of parents and kids as to why kids use alcohol and other drugs brings out an interesting point. The kids' explanations point **inward;** kids choose to use because something inside them urges them that way: for example, curiosity, desire for thrills. It's a personal choice. The parents' explanations point **outward,** to something or someone outside the youngster: the school, classmates, peer pressure.

Why do we think the way we do? How correct are our explanations? Our kids' explanations? What do these explanations imply? First, we may be unconsciously taking the easy way out: it's always convenient to have a clear, simple explanation and to blame someone else. Parents really are convinced of the explanations they give. I know, because I've worked with families who have sold their homes, changed schools, even moved their families to a different part of the country in a vain attempt to find an **environment** that would insulate their kids from outside influences that expose them to alcohol and other drugs.

Moreover, there's no denying the power of outside influences. Kids are influenced by an undisciplined school environment, by their peer group, by media idols, and so on. But to attribute their decisions totally or primarily to outside influences is clearly an exaggeration, and the implications of that view are quite ominous.

It sees our kids as helpless pawns in the grip of huge, uncontrollable forces—an attitude our kids can easily pick up from us. Insofar as we influence them that way, we're enablers who encourage them to believe it's useless to fight alcohol or other drugs.

It encourages us to throw up our hands in despair. After all, what can we do in the face of such odds—a world where everyone and everything seems to be controlling us and our kids? If we can't really do anything, why waste our time and energy trying? It's another way of being enablers.

Furthermore, it seems unreasonable to dismiss out of hand our kids' own explanations of their conduct, especially when those explanations aren't given under pressure. One interesting discovery made by researchers in the field of chemical dependence confirms kids' claims that they make free, personal choices about alcohol and other drugs. Researchers have discovered that kids often deliberately switch to another peer group so they can be with kids who have made the same decision as they have about using or not using alcohol and other drugs. This freely chosen switch indicates strongly that our kids are not simply putty in the hands of their peers.

All in all, the evidence indicates that kids do indeed, to a great extent, weigh the pros and cons of their own situation and make free, personal choices about using alcohol and other drugs.

The implications for us are quite clear and very encouraging. If neither we nor our kids are in the hands of external forces beyond control, then we and our kids can be in control of our own lives, make our own choices about alcohol and other drugs. We parents can structure our family life along lines that will equip us to help our kids stay away from alcohol and other drugs. Future chapters will flesh out this encouraging view.

Which Drugs Kids Use

Kids today are exposed to a far greater variety of drugs, including alcoholic drinks, than we were at their age. So it isn't easy for us to learn just the basics we need to know.

But we need to know them. The following is a list of the most common kinds of drugs that kids today are using, as well as the more important information about each. I want to point out that all these drugs have one thing in common: **They all affect the chemistry of our minds.** Therefore, they're often referred to as **mind-altering chemicals.**

Checklist of Drugs

Alcohol

Forms Used: wine, wine coolers, beer, malt liquors, distilled liquor, e.g., whiskey, vodka, gin, etc.

Method of Use: drinking, in which the chemical is absorbed through the lining of the stomach.

Quick Facts:

- Beverage alcohol is a central nervous system depressant.
- Alcohol is the most widely abused drug in our society.
- It can cause intoxication, unconsciousness, or even death.
- It is as potent as many illegal drugs.
- Drinking and driving are a particularly dangerous mix.
- Alcohol can cause severe damage to the developing fetus.
- Young people are much more vulnerable than adults to alcohol's physical and psychological risks.
- 45-50% of adolescents who are victims of violent death have been drinking alcohol before the fatal event.
- Alcohol is the intoxicant of choice for teens.
- Teenagers can and do become alcoholics.
- When parents allow their underage child to use alcohol for any reason, the chances that young person will develop problems with alcohol or other drugs increases threefold.
- More than one out of four high school seniors report binge drinking (5 or more drinks in a row) in the past *two weeks.*

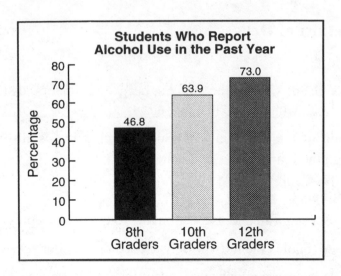

Tobacco

Forms Used: cigarettes, snuff, chewing tobacco, or cigars.

Method of Use: smoking, in which the chemical is absorbed through the lungs. Chewing or puffing (as in cigars or pipes) in which the chemical is absorbed through the lining of the mouth and throat.

Quick Facts:

- Tobacco is one of the most widely used psychoactive drugs in the world.

- Tobacco contains nicotine, a central nervous system stimulant.

- Tobacco contains thousands of other chemical compounds, many of which are known to cause cancer.

- Use of tobacco can cause heart disease, lung cancer, emphysema, and many other fatal disorders.

- Use of smokeless tobacco can be as dangerous as smoking.

- Tobacco can harm the developing fetus.

- Tobacco smoke can be harmful for nonsmokers who breathe it.

- Use of tobacco by young people is considered to be a "gateway" to other forms of drug use.

- Nicotine dependence is the most common serious medical problem in the United States.

- U.S. teens purchase over a billion dollars worth of tobacco products each year, generating a profit of approximately $270 million annually for tobacco companies.

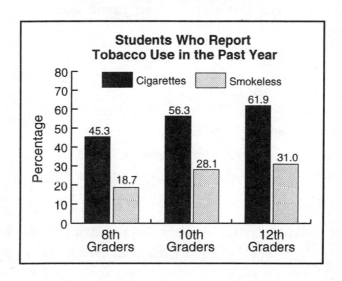

Cannabis (Marijuana)

Forms Used: hand-rolled marijuana cigarettes (joints), loose marijuana (smoked in pipes), hashish (condensed forms of marijuana that look like small balls of tar or dark clay).

Methods of Use: smoking, whereby the chemical is absorbed through the lungs. Eating (usually by mixing marijuana or hashish into a food, e.g., brownies or cake) in which the chemical is absorbed through the lining of the stomach.

Quick Facts:

Cannabis is the most frequently used illicit drug in the United States.

The average potency of marijuana has increased considerably since the 1970s.

- Cannabis has some of the same effects as depressants, stimulants, and hallucinogens.

- Cannabis alters the heart rate and can cause anxiety, panic attacks, or paranoia.

- Marijuana cigarettes yield almost four times as much tar as tobacco, creating high risk of lung damage.

- Cannabis can harm the developing fetus.

- Cannabis use impairs short-term memory, thinking, concentration, attention span, and physical coordination. (Memory lapses can last for up to six-weeks after the last use of the drug.)

- Marijuana smoke contains carcinogens and toxic particles that can lead to bronchitis, emphysema, and lung cancer.

- Chronic marijuana use has been associated with reduced sperm count in males.

- Marijuana use among young people has been increasing significantly since 1992.

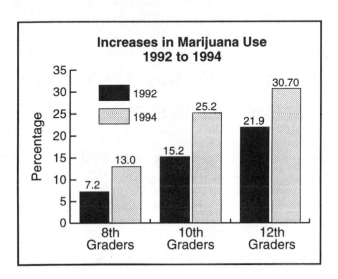

Inhalants

Forms Used: These include a long list of materials that either emit or propel a gas that contains intoxicating fumes. Some of the more popular substances include: model airplane glue, gasoline, paint or lacquer thinners, typewriter correction fluid *(White Out),* cleaning fluids, nail polish remover, lighter fluid, nitrous oxide (used as a sedative by dentists or as a propellant in whipped cream aerosols), butyl nitrate (Originally sold as a locker room deodorizer under the trade name *Locker Room.* Now sold in drug paraphernalia shops as *Bolt, Rush, QuickSilver, or Highball.)* markers, or anything in an aerosol can (e.g., deodorant, *Pam,* spray paint, etc.).

Methods Used: The substance is usually placed in a small plastic or paper bag, and the fumes are inhaled by placing the opening of the bag over the mouth and nose. Occasionally the fumes are inhaled by holding a rag or handkerchief to the mouth and nose (sniffing or huffing). Sometimes liquids are inhaled by sniffing the fumes directly from the container (e.g., gasoline).

Quick Facts:

- Most inhalants are central nervous system depressants.

- Many people (especially young people) don't think of inhalants as drugs.

- Moderate use of these drugs can result in intoxication similar to that caused by alcohol.

- Most inhalants contain many ingredients, some of which are highly toxic.

- People can become dependent on inhalants.

- Driving under the influence of inhalants is hazardous.

- Inhalants can harm the developing fetus.

- Inhalants are most frequently abused by youths ninth grade and younger. (Many first try inhalants when they are only 7 or 8 years old.)

- Because it is impossible to control or even estimate the dose, many fatalities have been directly associated with inhalant use.

- Chronic exposure to inhalants can cause permanent brain damage.

- Long term use of inhalants will harm the lungs, liver, and kidneys.

- Chromosomal abnormalities have been found in youths who sniff glue.

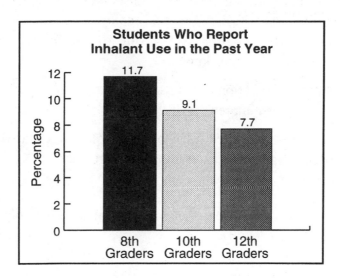

Hallucinogens

Forms Used: LSD (lysergic acid diethyl amide), PCP (phencyclidine or "angel dust") psilocybin, mescaline. LSD is usually found in the form of tiny cylindrical tablets, tiny gelatin squares, or absorbed on small pieces of paper (which are chewed to extract the chemical). PCP can be found in the form of a powder, a liquid, granules, capsules, or tablets.

Methods Used: Most hallucinogens are taken orally; however, PCP is also frequently dusted onto tobacco or marijuana and smoked.

Quick Facts:

- Hallucinogens alter mood, thought , perception, and brain function.

- Some of these drugs also cause stimulation of the central nervous system.

- The hallucinogen LSD is one of the most potent psychoactive drugs known.

- Street preparations of these drugs are rarely pure and can produce unpredictable effects.

- People sometimes have brief or prolonged adverse psychological reactions to hallucinogen use.

- Hallucinogens can harm the developing fetus.

- Driving while under the influence of a hallucinogen is hazardous.

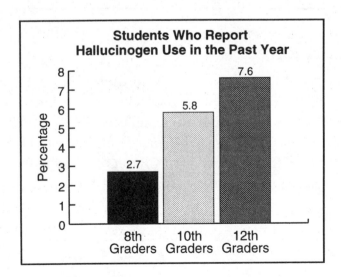

Cocaine

Forms Used: cocaine hydrochloride, a white powder that is water soluble, or *cocaine* freebase (commonly referred to as crack or crack cocaine), which is usually sold in the form of rocks or chunks that are odorless and usually off-white in color. Crack is usually sold at a lower cost per-dose than pure cocaine.

Methods Used: Cocaine hydrochloride is usually snorted or dissolved in water and injected directly into the veins of the user. Crack cocaine is usually smoked.

Quick Facts:

- Cocaine is a powerful central nervous system stimulant.

- It produces a short-lived sense of euphoria, the length of which depends mainly on the route of administration.

- Heavy use of the drug can be physically harmful.

- Crack is a potent form of the drug that is highly addictive.

- Exposure to the drug can harm the developing fetus.

- Cocaine users are at increased risk of infectious disease.

- One-time use of cocaine can produce seizures, respiratory arrest, or cardiac arrest and high fever, which can result in death.

- The intense high from crack cocaine lasts less than 10 minutes, resulting in an intense craving to avoid the anxiety that follows. This cycle results in an extremely high rate of addiction.

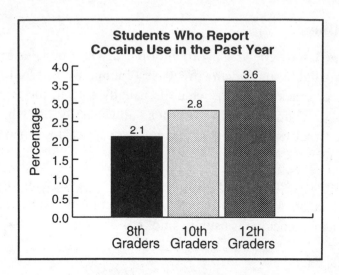

Other Stimulants

Forms Used: amphetamine, methamphetamine, dextroamphetamine, benzphetamine, and crystal amphetamine (ice).

Methods Used: The most common method of using amphetamines is oral ingestion; however, some regular users of amphetamines inject the drug. The primary method for using crystal amphetamine (ice) is by smoking.

Quick Facts:

- Amphetamines are strong central nervous system stimulants.

- Heavy doses or long-term use of amphetamines can lead to severe anxiety, malnutrition, paranoia, and death.

- Amphetamines are particularly dangerous for people with high blood pressure, heart disease, diabetes, or thyroid disease.

- Amphetamine use during pregnancy can harm the developing fetus.

- Driving while using amphetamines is hazardous.

- Use of amphetamines can reduce a person's resistance to disease.

- Chronic users of amphetamines may develop a condition resembling paranoid schizophrenia. (Symptoms include hallucinations, fearful delusions, and compulsive or repetitive behavior.)

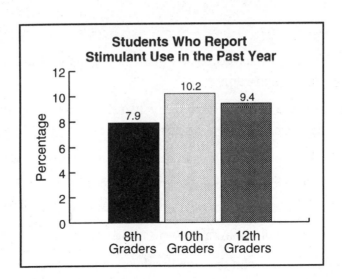

Opiates

Forms Used: heroin, morphine, opium, methadone, codeine, oxycodone, hydromorphone, ropoxyphene, meperidine, and pentazocine.

Methods Used: With the exception of heroin and opium, most opiates are taken orally. Opium and heroin freebase can be smoked. Heroin is often injected intravenously by long term addicts; however, with the risk of AIDS from unsterilized needles many addicts have begun to snort the drug (the drug is absorbed through the linings of the nose).

Quick Facts:

- Opiates, or narcotic analgesics, are drugs that cause sedation and euphoria.

- Opiates are used medically to relieve pain, suppress cough, and control diarrhea.

- Some opiates, such as heroin, have no medical use, and any possession or use is illicit.

- Overdose can cause death by respiratory depression.

- Opiates can impair a person's ability to drive.

- These drugs can damage the developing fetus.

- Opiate abuse is linked with the spread of AIDS.

- It can be hazardous to mix opiates with other drugs.

(Heroin use for all grades is less than 1% of the students surveyed; other opiate use in the past year by high school seniors was 3.3% of the students surveyed.)

Other Sedatives

Forms Used: barbiturates, tranquilizers, methaqualone (Quaalude or "ludes"), benzodiazepines (e.g., diazepam and chlordiazepoxide).

Methods Used: Most of these drugs are in the form of prescription medicines and are taken orally; however, they can also be taken intravenously.

Quick Facts:

- All sedatives are a central nervous system depressant.
- Sedatives are particularly dangerous when combined with any other form of depressant, such as alcohol.
- Driving under the influence of sedatives is dangerous.
- Sedatives can harm the developing fetus.
- Sedative users often find themselves addicted to their prescription drug because of rapidly developing tolerance to the effects and the high degree of cross-tolerance among many tranquilizers and barbiturates.

Barbiturates are:

- prescribed to treat anxiety, sleeplessness, and to control seizures.
- dangerous in high doses, often causing death.
- potentially fatal when barbiturate addicts attempt to go through withdrawal without medical supervision.

Tranquilizers are:

- prescribed to treat anxiety and insomnia.
- among the most commonly prescribed drugs in the world.

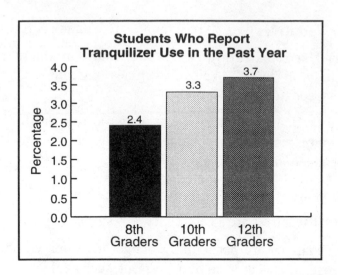

Designer Drugs

Designer drugs, also known as analogs, are synthetic chemical modifications of commonly abused drugs (usually amphetamines or opiates) which are manufactured in illegal labs. Modification of the drug serves two purposes:

- In the 1980s it was difficult to prosecute the manufacturers of these drugs because technically the compounds are slightly different than the illegal chemical they were designed to replicate. In 1986 federal drug laws were rewritten to classify any analogs of a controlled substance as an illegal drug under Schedule I of the Controlled Substances Act.

- Some of the designer drugs are more potent and less expensive than the original drug, therefore yielding huge profits for the illicit producers and distributors.

Forms Used: Designer amphetamines are commonly produced as MDMA or "ecstasy" and MDEA or "eve." Designer opiates often take the form of the powerful narcotic anesthetic *fentanyl.* The designer form of this narcotic is often referred to as "China White." Most of the designer drugs take the form of a white or off-white powder.

Methods Used: Designer drugs may be taken orally, intravenously, smoked, or snorted.

Quick Facts:

- Designer drugs, and the impurities that are often in them, can be very dangerous.

- These drugs are often much more potent than the drugs they are designed to imitate.

- Drugs that are chemically similar to controlled substances are illegal.

- Because of inconsistencies in production and dose, any use of designer drugs should be considered potentially fatal or debilitating.

To find out more information on alcohol and other drugs please refer to the source for the Quick Facts in this section, *Mind Altering Drugs: A Guide to the History, Uses and Effects of Psychoactive Drugs,* Wisconsin Clearinghouse, P.O. Box 1468, Madison, WI 53701 1-800-322-1468. Copyright 1992, Wisconsin Clearinghouse, Board of Regents of the University of Wisconsin System.

Statistics on the incidence of use are from *The National Survey Results on Drug Use from the Monitoring the Future Study,* 1975-1994, *Volume 1 Secondary School Students,* (in preparation) Johnston, O'Malley, and Bachman, National Institute on Drug Abuse, Rockville Maryland, 1995 (Data on tobacco were unreleased at the point of publication; therefore data on tobacco reflect information from students collected in 1993.)

At What Age Kids Use Alcohol or Other Drugs

We must accept the fact that kids are beginning to use alcohol and other drugs at much earlier ages then ever. This may be due in part to the fact that adolescence is actually starting earlier than ever before. Adolescence, once synonymous with the teenage years, is now considered to begin as early as age 9 or 10. Research of the past 15 years consistently shows that secondary sex characteristics, usually considered an indicator of the beginning of puberty, are appearing 18 to 24 months earlier than in previous decades.

Why this earlier onset of adolescence? We're not sure; experts in different fields give different answers.

- Health-care professionals cite **improved health-care resources** that have eliminated many childhood diseases.

- Psychologists and social workers cite kids' **increased capacity for and demand for independence**—a demand caused by outside influences such as TV programs aimed at kids and by their exposure to daycare.

- Family counselors cite **parental pressure.** Parents' eagerness to "give kids the best" means that we sometimes indulge them with activities and materials that actually rob them of their childhood. Thumb through an upscale magazine such as *Child* and you'll see pierced ears, designer clothes, cosmetics, and off-the-road vehicles depicted as a "normal" part of childhood. As one first-grade teacher lamented, "You'd think someone would finally realize that all-night slumber parties for kindergartners might well lead to all-night keggers for sixth graders."

Whatever the reason, kids are growing up earlier than ever before. It's hard to say whether this is good or bad; probably some of both. But one undeniably negative consequence is that kids are now exposed to choices about chemical use at a much earlier age.

There are no reliable measurements of when kids younger than sixth-grade age start to use alcohol or other drugs. But some isolated research gives us a hint.

A 1991 *Weekly Reader* study indicates that grade school children report substantial peer pressure to try alcohol as early as fourth grade. Thirty-five percent of fourth graders say they felt some to a lot of peer pressure to try beer, wine, or distilled spirits.

The study goes on to say that the proportion of fourth, fifth, and sixth graders who believe that "few or many" kids their age in their town have tried alcohol increases by grade level, ranging from about 79% of 4th graders to 93% of 6th graders.*

There are more accurate data on kids beyond grade-school years. According to the *Monitoring the Future Study 1994,* which surveyed 8th, 10th, and 12th graders, the 10th graders (The Class of 1995) reported that they began using alcohol, marijuana, and inhalants in the following grades:

---

*The Weekly Reader National Survey on Drugs and Alcohol, Terry Borton, Ed. D., editor. (Middletown, Connecticut: Field Publications. 1991).

Grade in which drug was first used	Alcohol	Marijuana	Inhalants
6th grade	11.2%	2.3%	2.2%
7th/8th grade	24.7%	6.8%	5.0%
9th grade	19.7%	6.9%	2.9%
10th grade	15.9%	6.5%	2.8%
11th grade	10.1%	7.5%	3.1%
12th grade	5.4%	5.3%	1.4%
Never Used	13.0%	64.7%	82.6%

As we study this chart we notice that by ninth grade over 55% of our kids will have used some type of mind-altering chemical. So it seems reasonable to assume that the other 45% reporting no alcohol or other drug use will nevertheless have had to make choices about chemical use or at least will have been exposed to friends who have chosen to use. The message is clear: our kids must be prepared to deal with choices about alcohol and other drug use well before their **ninth-grade year.** Most experts agree that **somewhere during their fourth-grade year** a substantial number of young people must make this major decision. To ignore these realities and to do nothing to prepare our kids for dealing with these realities means we're burying our heads in the sand—another form of enabling.

Where Kids Do and Don't Use Alcohol and Other Drugs

Adolescents consistently report that the most common places and events for alcohol and drug use are:

- with friends
- at parties
- in cars

Those same adolescents report that a common situation, place, or time for alcohol use but not for use of other drugs such as marijuana is:

- with a date
- with adults (defined as persons over 30)
- at home
- after 4:00 P.M.

Adolescents consistently report that alcohol and other drugs are not commonly used:

- alone
- at school (however, significantly more adolescents using marijuana reported using it at school as compared to adolescents who reported using alcohol at school).

How Kids Use Alcohol and Other Drugs

To understand how kids use, let's look at Mike, age 16, whom I met during his treatment for chemical dependence. Before seventh grade Mike was an excellent student and athlete. But then he embarked on a course that took him through what we now recognize as the typical three phases that lead to chemical dependence.

Phase I: Learning the Mood Swing

During seventh grade Mike is introduced to alcohol at the home of his best friend. They split three beers. That year Mike and his friend continue to sneak beers together about twice per month.

During this initial use Mike learns that alcohol is fun. He learns that every time he uses the drug it makes him feel better. He learns that he can control how he feels by how much alcohol he uses. He finds that afterward he feels no ill effects, experiences no problems.

Feeling intoxicated begins to be important to Mike. He's using alcohol because:

- It's fun—he likes the feeling.
- He's curious.
- He likes to take risks.

Phase II: Seeking the Mood Swing

Mike enters eighth grade. During a Boy Scout campout he and four others get really drunk and really sick. Mike's parents are notified, and he's grounded for two weeks. He feels terrible for having let down his parents, his family, and his Boy Scout leader.

He doesn't use for six weeks. Then after the eighth-grade Homecoming football game, some friends invite him to a party. He drinks and remembers how much fun it is to be intoxicated. He feels he's really been missing something these last six weeks.

He begins hanging out occasionally with a new group of friends, including some ninth and tenth graders. They drink more frequently and use greater amounts than his other friends. Two or three in the group also smoke marijuana. Mike now uses marijuana (as well as beer) once or twice a week. Also, he's now made better plans for keeping his parents from finding out. After all, he couldn't let them down again.

Mike's reasons for using alcohol and other drugs now are:

* Most of his friends use.
* Life isn't as much fun without it.
* Why not? It really doesn't cause any problems.

Phase III: Harmful Dependence

Mike has now moved into his sophomore year of high school. Getting loaded has become a lot more important to him. If he has to spend a weekend at home with his family he feels extremely restless and fidgety. His parents describe him as being like a caged animal.

Mike has made significant changes in his life because of his alcohol and other drug use.

* His grades have slipped from a B+ average to C-.
* He's quit the football team but is still playing hockey once in awhile with friends.
* His tolerance for alcohol has grown.
    - He now regularly drinks four to eight beers at a sitting.
    - He's developing a real taste for vodka.
    - He's tried marijuana and some white crosses (street amphetamines) but really doesn't like either as much as alcohol.

- His values have changed to accommodate his alcohol and other drug use. He thinks nothing of lying to his parents to cover up his activities.

- His friends now include a number of older kids and young adults. Some of the 19-to-20 year olds are heavy users (by Mike's standards): He's seen them snort cocaine. He once smoked crack with one of them.

- Mike's girlfriend has dropped him; she told him she was worried about his use.

- His parents have become very concerned about his drop in grades, change of friends, and secretive behavior. He never wants to be with the family, and he won't tell them where he's going.

- All attempts at controlling him have failed. While grounded, he sneaks out his window after midnight. His parents are at their wits' end.

- Mike keeps people at a distance by pretending everything is okay. When confronted with a problem he makes the problem seem insignificant. (We call it minimizing.)

- When pushed he becomes belligerent and angry and usually stalks off.

Getting high has become Mike's number one priority in life. He's sacrificed his relationship with his girlfriend, his family, his honesty, his integrity, and he's compromised his athletic ability.

Mike's reasons for use are now:
- to escape
- to avoid responsibilities
- to avoid problems (many of them caused by his use).

Mike is referred for treatment during the summer before his eleventh grade as a result of a breaking-and-entering charge. He was intoxicated at the time, but he doesn't really believe he has a problem. How could he not see the truth? Because by now his denial of any alcohol or other drug problem has become a full-scale delusion: a condition in which a person is out of touch with reality, but by that very fact is unaware of the delusion.

By this time, Mike has reached the stage where getting loaded is the only thing he can count on to make himself feel good.

Phase IV: Using to Feel Normal

If Mike were to continue to use he would eventually move to this last stage of chemical use. During this stage his use would probably begin having numerous consequences such as:

- physical addiction
- overdose
- severe emotional distress
- severe legal problems
- suicide attempts.

The reasons for continuing to use in Phase IV include:

- to feel normal
- to avoid physical and psychological pain
- to be able to function without withdrawal symptoms: extreme shakiness, nausea/vomiting, paranoia, agitation, or weakness.

Summary

In this chapter we've covered the what, when, why, where, and how of adolescents' use of alcohol and other drugs. As our kids reach the third and fourth grades, many of them will be confronted with choices about whether to use alcohol or other drugs. As they make those decisions they'll need us to be there for them as resources, guides, authorities. If we don't have adequate information we run the risk of letting them down.

In its initial stages alcohol or other drug use is clearly a free personal choice that kids make. Our goal, as parents interested in prevention, is to help them make responsible choices that lead to long-term success. One of the most critical ways we can help our kids avoid problems with alcohol or other drugs is found in how we communicate with our kids about our beliefs and values. Unfortunately, young people receive multiple messages regarding this crucial topic. We adults can best help young people avoid problems when our messages are clear and consistent.

The next chapter focuses on the problems that our unclear messages create for our kids, and ways we can avoid the pitfalls of mixed messages regarding alcohol and other drugs.

3

Avoiding Mixed Messages

No matter how educated we become as parents, the message we give young people regarding alcohol and other drug use is critical. In a survey completed by Minnesota students, students who were non-users were asked why they didn't use alcohol or other drugs. Consistently, one of the top reasons given by students was that they believed their parents would be upset. Obviously, how we feel, and more important, our ability and willingness to communicate directly to our kids how we feel make a difference.

Why We Give Mixed Messages About Alcohol

The fact is young people are significant consumers of alcoholic beverages. A recent study by the U.S. Inspector General shows that 35% of the wine coolers consumed in the United States were by junior and senior high school students.

At the Johnson Institute, we surveyed over 100,000 students from across the country. During the pilot phase of the research, we asked students if their parents **approved** of them using alcohol. The response was remarkably consistent: well over 95% of the students reported that their parents didn't approve of them using alcohol. As we continued to develop the survey, we changed the question to get information we believed would be more useful to parents. We changed the question to "Do your parents **allow** you to use alcohol?" The students' response to this subtly different question was dramatically different from the earlier question. When the question was changed from "Do they **approve**?" to "Do they **allow**?" we found that more than two out of three parents of tenth graders actually allow their kids to use alcohol in certain situations. ("At a celebration" or "at family parties," were the most notable situations in which students reported their parents allowed them to use alcohol.)

In talking with parents during parent education seminars around the country, I have had the opportunity to question parents why they and other parents they know allow their kids to drink, even though they clearly disapprove. Their answers might sound familiar to you. Parents tell me:

- They believe that if they don't allow their kids to drink at home, their kids will be more likely to drink in less safe environments (in cars, at parties, etc.).

- They believe that by letting their kids use beer or wine coolers they will prevent them from using other drugs they believe to be more dangerous, such as marijuana, cocaine, LSD, etc.

- They believe that because of overwhelming peer pressure—which they think kids feel—their kids will be excluded from social activities and will be less popular or have fewer friends if they don't let their kids drink.

Mixed Messages Cause Problems

What happens when we allow our kids to use alcohol? Despite the fact that most parents who allow their kids to drink are motivated by the best of intentions, the results are frequently anything but positive. The chart below shows marked contrast between students who report that their parents allow them to use alcohol and students whose parents give a firm no-use message regarding alcohol use.

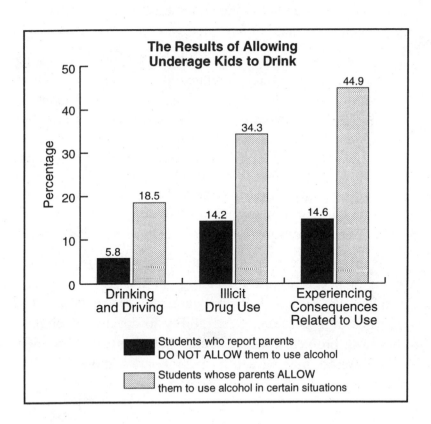

The evidence is compelling. When parents bargain on the issue of underage alcohol consumption, their kids are:

- More than three times more likely to be a casualty of drinking and driving. (5.8% of kids who are *not* allowed to drink versus 18.5% of kids who *are* allowed to drink report drinking and driving or being in a car where someone else is drinking and driving.)

- Nearly two and a half times more likely to use an illicit drug. (A drug that is illegal for adults, such as marijuana or crack cocaine.)

- More than three times more likely to report experiencing a consequence directly related to their use of alcohol or other drugs. (For example, problems with friends or difficulty in school.)

While many parents fear their kids will have no one to socialize with if they don't allow them to use alcohol, the fact is that nearly one out of four juniors and seniors report that they do not use any form of alcohol or other drugs. In 9th and 10th grade, those numbers are closer to one in three who don't use.

As mentioned earlier, adults have typically exaggerated the effects of peer pressure on young people. At the Johnson Institute we've analyzed whether vulnerability to peer pressure translates into increased vulnerability to develop alcohol or other drug problems. We've found that, contrary to popular opinion, direct messages from parents are a more powerful influence on kids' choices than peer pressure.

Mixed Messages from the Media

Selling alcohol and tobacco is a big business, and the sales effort is supported by massive advertising budgets. Tobacco manufacturers spend $3.27 billion a year promoting their products, and beer and wine producers invest an additional $1 billion advertising alcoholic beverages. Many of these ads are misleading and are designed to appeal specifically to young people.

The media is a powerful influence on young people. American children spend an average of three to four hours per day in front of the TV, with another twenty to thirty hours per week listening to the radio. However, the electronic media is not the only place where tobacco and alcohol are promoted. Cigarettes rank as the most heavily advertised products on billboards and the second most promoted product in magazines.

Clearly, advertising increases the appetite of the consumer for the product. As one advertising executive noted in a *Newsweek* article, "If greater advertising over time doesn't generate greater profits, there's something seriously wrong with the fellows who make up the budgets."[1] Not only does advertising work, but it seems to work better on young people. The National Science Foundation reported," It is clear from the available evidence that television does influence children . . . advertising is at least moderately successful in creating a positive attitude toward and the desire for the products advertised . . . younger viewers . . .appear to be the most vulnerable."[2]

Consider the following:

- The most heavily advertised cigarettes in the U.S. (Marlboro and Camel) are the brand of choice of almost 90% of the teen smokers, while the same brands capture less than 30% of the adult market. (Many would argue that these two brands in particular target young people with their promotional message.)[3]

- A study of Maryland 8-to-12 year olds found they were able to name more brands of beer than names of American presidents.[4]

- In Norway the prevalence of 13-to-15 year old smokers fell from 17% to 10% after an advertising ban on cigarettes was imposed.[5]

- A study published in 1991 found that 6 year olds were as likely to recognize "Old Joe," the mascot for Camel cigarettes as the Mousketeer logo for the Disney Channel.[6]

Clearly, the messages children receive about alcohol and other drugs are vitally important to the choices they will eventually make. We, as parents, must search for creative ways to consistently and firmly hold the media—and the business groups they represent—responsible for the messages they deliver to our children regarding this critical issue. It can be extremely difficult for kids to "say no" to underage drinking or tobacco use, when their favorite mascot is consistently encouraging them to "say yes" to Budweiser or Camels.

Summary

The fact is that we adults are powerful. As parents, business people, educators, or journalists, we are responsible for the information our young people get regarding alcohol and other drugs. Too frequently the message is mixed. On the one hand they hear us saying that we don't approve of drugs, but on the other hand, they continue to get permission to use certain drugs in certain situations. The fact is that kids rely on us for consistent and sound information that reflects clear limits and values regarding this critical choice. Too frequently we let our kids down by taking the path of least resistance, as we try to win their approval by being soft or by laughing at the popular commercial with its mixed message and inaccurate information about alcohol and tobacco. We must always remember that our kids are intently listening to the words we say and the values our behavior communicates. The power we have as parents and adults in the community wields much more impact on kids than many of us have been willing to admit.

In chapters 4 and 5 we will explore a framework that clearly spells out how we can use our power as parents more effectively without interfering with our child's emerging sense of responsibility and healthy independence.

Endnotes

[1] R.J. Samuelson, "The End of Free Advertising?" *Newsweek,* August 19, 1991, 40.

[2] "Research on the Effects of Television Advertising on Children: A Review of the Literature and Recommendations for Future Research," (Washington, D.C.: National Science Foundation, 1977).

[3] Victor C. Strasburger, M.D., "Adolescents, Drugs, and the Media," *Adolescent Medicine: State of the Art Reviews,* 4:2, June 1993.

[4] "Kids Are as Aware of Booze as President," news release, Center for Science in the Public Interest, (Washington, D.C.: 1988).

[5] A. Vickers, "Why Cigarette Advertising Should Be Banned," *British Medical Journal,* 304:1195-1196, 1992.

[6] P.M. Fischer, M.P. Schwart, J.W. Richards, et al. "Brand Logo Recognition by Children Aged 3 to 6 Years: Mickey Mouse and Old Joe the Camel," *JAMA,* 266:3145-3153, 1991.

4

A Job Description
for Parents

A parent couple, Larry and Anne, can give us some basic
insights into the meat of this chapter.

Larry came from a family known for strict discipline.
Rules were numerous and never bent; punishments were
harsh. Kids were "seen but not heard." Family members
seldom openly expressed their feelings, whether of anger,
enthusiasm, or affection. Anne came from a family in which
parenting was the polar opposite of what Larry grew up with.
The kids practically raised themselves. There were almost no
rules, and the few they did have were seldom enforced, or
were enforced inconsistently. Family members were quite open
about expressing their feelings, whether that meant showing
anger or sharing affection with hugs and words of praise.

When Anne's and Larry's first child, Matt, was 18 months
old and began asserting himself, their vastly different views on
parenting also asserted themselves. Larry typically responded
to Matt's tantrums with punishment that went on till the child

gave in. Anne typically ignored Matt's outbursts with "He'll get over it" and would simply try to wait out the storm.

These opposite views made for greater and greater problems as Matt grew up. When he was in sixth grade his temper tantrums and angry outbursts became common, and he often skipped school and ignored curfew. Larry's complaint to Anne was "If you'd just support me in setting up some rules and enforcing them with consequences, he'd know what's expected of him and he'd shape up. He **needs** that kind of control. We've got to show him who's boss." Anne's answer was "Matt needs room to breathe. You're on him all the time. I think he skips school because he needs relief from all this tension. You just don't know how to let go; after all, he's no infant."

Taking Charge versus Letting Go

The story of Anne and Larry illustrates a crucial problem that all parents must face: Do we "take charge," or do we "let go?" As you might expect, the answer isn't simple—but the question can be answered sensibly, and that's what this chapter is about. What **is** immediately clear is that parents **must** agree on their basic approach to parenting and then on some clear guidelines for implementing their approach. I'm calling those guidelines **a job description for parents.** Once you've learned these guidelines and how to use them, you'll be more at ease as parents, and your kids will be more at ease, too, because they'll be living in a well-balanced, happy family, in an environment that gives them both the security and the freedom they need—**security** and **freedom** that result when parents have learned both how to "take charge" and how to "let go."

From Control to Freedom

Many parents have found the following simple image helpful as they try to arrive at that delicate balance between taking charge and letting go.

If a young bird is to learn to fly on its own, it needs a certain kind of home base: one that's firm and stable, to give it **security;** and one that's generously sized and not too self-enclosed, to give it **freedom** to flap its wings, strengthen them, and start short trial flights, even at the cost of a few rather hard landings that shake it up but don't cause any serious injury.

This image of the kind of home the fledgling needs if it's to grow up and learn to fly (and eventually to leave both nest and parents) clarifies a two-pronged truth about what happens to the parent-child relationship as our kids grow up. When they're mere infants we quite naturally and necessarily exercise almost total control to make them secure. They're completely dependent on us: for food, shelter, cleanliness, and safety from dozens of possible dangers. But as they grow older, two facts emerge. First, **they become more able to do more things on their own:** feed and dress and defend themselves, and much later on make major decisions about what friends to associate with, what activities to get into or avoid, what life work to settle into. Second, as our youngsters become more able to take care of themselves, **we're simply less able to exercise control.**

As we absorb this double truth, it becomes clear that as **our kids grow up we must constantly keep redefining our roles as parents.**

From Freedom to Responsibility

An important part of redefining our roles as parents consists of realizing that **freedom calls for responsibility.** It's a truth that must become a reality both to us parents and to our kids.

For us it means that as our kids demonstrate increasing ability to be responsible for themselves and to others, we must not only let them exercise responsibility but must positively encourage them to do so. Early on, it might be only a matter of letting them decide which candy bar to buy, which dress to wear; later, whether to get into gymnastics or soccer, whether to try out for the class play or learn the flute. Whatever the choices are, insofar as we make all those choices for our kids, we're not learning to let go, and we're failing to let them grow up to learn what responsibility means. But insofar as we encourage them to make choices in matters they can handle at their stage of development, we're gradually learning to loosen our tight grip on them, and we're giving them opportunities to test and strengthen their wings for confident solo flight later on.

For our kids it means that they must learn that if they want freedom to make their own choices, to do it their way, they must also take responsibility for those choices—must learn that actions have consequences, and that when they choose the action, they're choosing to accept the consequences. It's not hard to see how important such a responsible attitude will be when our kids come to the really big choices such as "What group do I run around with?" and "Do I use alcohol or other drugs, or don't I?" (In the next chapter we'll go much deeper into the issue of letting kids take on responsibilities.)

The Need for Parental Consensus on Principles

Before we go on to discuss our job description for parents, I must repeat for emphasis a point I mentioned earlier in passing: **It's absolutely essential that parents agree on these guidelines.** Such an agreement is indispensable because it gives our kids a secure environment—secure because it's consistent and therefore **predictable.** You needn't be afraid that these guidelines will straitjacket you, though; if you hold onto them, you can easily work out many variations that suit your own family, as countless other successful parents have done and continue to do.

A Time-tested Job Description for Parents

The following guidelines have come from parents themselves—parents I've worked with over the years. I know these guidelines work because I've **seen** them work in the daily lives of hundreds of families. Furthermore, as a professional family counselor I can assure you that they're down-to-earth applications of sound parenting principles. As you apply these guidelines to your own family, I urge you to keep checking your progress in light of two of the most basic of them.

- **Our primary goal** in parenting is to prepare our children for dealing with the real world.

- **The methods we use** to prepare them for that real world must always be evaluated in terms of how well they meet our children's deepest human needs such as self-esteem, self-respect, self-reliance, and deeply satisfying relationships with others.

All good parenting must pass that double test.

Let's start this job description for parents by discussing a duty that has perhaps been somewhat neglected in recent years: that of setting limits for children.

Setting Limits

The smallest infant is geared to exploring the big, mysterious world around it, and of course parents should encourage what will become a lifelong quest. Experiencing colors, sounds, shapes, textures, and smells, crawling to new, wonderful places—all this is part of the adventure of growing up. But always the parents have to set limits. We don't let the baby put its hand on a hot stove to learn what heat means; we don't let it crawl outside in zero weather to learn what cold is. We set limits. Inevitably, youngsters test those limits, and more and more so as they come into adolescence and reach for true independence. To an adolescent, limits exist to be tested. How serious are Mom and Dad about the jobs they give me around the house and yard? About how much money I can spend? About what I can or can't wear? About what time I have to be in at night? About using the car? About my using alcohol or other drugs? How far can I really go? And what happens if I go too far? But no matter how much adolescents question or test the limits we set, we must indeed set them. The real world we all have to face is hemmed in with limits of all kinds; the adolescent who hasn't learned to accept reasonable limits in everyday home life isn't likely to accept them in dealing with decisions about alcohol and other drugs either, because the unspoken principle has been "Do whatever you like."

But **how** do we set limits? I suggest three criteria. Set limits that are **clear** and **appropriate,** and **enforce** them.

Set Clear Limits

The adolescent (this does apply especially to adolescents!) who for some reason can't distinguish what's appropriate dress for the beach from what's appropriate for church or synagogue can suddenly turn into a razor-sharp, hair-splitting Madison Avenue attorney when parents establish limits that are open to even the slightest ambiguity. ("I know I'm supposed to finish my homework before I watch TV. But does that mean I can **never** watch before I finish it? **Never?** You didn't say **never.** I figured you must have meant usually, and this isn't a usual night; there's a playoff game.")

To tell the truth, parental limits sometimes **are** unclear because parents themselves haven't agreed on them. Parental agreement must come first. But then parents must express the limits in absolutely clear, specific terms that the youngster can understand. To test yourselves and your child, **write down** the limits, **discuss** them until the child agrees they're clear and can, if asked, **rephrase** them in his or her own words. ("Coming home an hour after the game is over" doesn't mean **starting** for home; it means **arriving** there. So we reword it to "arriving." "After the game is over" doesn't mean chatting in the gym for a half hour and then starting to count; it means being home an hour after the final buzzer.)

For additional insurance of clear communication, **post the limits** in a place where you and your child can easily review them, such as on the refrigerator, family bulletin board, or any other easily accessible place frequently used by all.

Set Appropriate Limits

Since no two kids are alike, limits must reflect your child's unique needs and capacities. Here are some areas to consider in deciding what's appropriate.

- **Age:** Kids often complain it isn't fair if they're not given the same freedom that an older brother or sister has. But parents shouldn't be swayed by that argument. Just explain that their time hasn't come but that it will— as they continue to prove they can handle greater freedom by showing maturity and a growing sense of responsibility in handling the privileges they already enjoy.

- **Trust earned:** We need to explain two points about trust to our kids.

    First, they must **earn** our trust. Here's why. When we trust people we somehow put ourselves in their hands, rely on them to do what's right. Before we do that, it only makes sense that they **show** us they're worthy of our trust; they have to **earn** our trust. Now, young children typically haven't had many opportunities to prove they're trustworthy. We **hope** they'll prove trustworthy, of course; but meantime, we'll be happy to trust them more and more as they **earn** our trust—for instance, by doing their chores without being told, and by coming home on time.

    Second, so our kids won't think that's a pretty harsh view of them, we need to explain a second point: **that trusting them and loving them are two different things.** We do love them. Loving them is a commitment we made from the start; it's a natural part of family life, an unwavering commitment from us, and we'll continue to love them no matter what they do. They don't have to earn our love; they already have it. But our trust—that's something they'll have to **earn,** and we hope they'll earn it.

- **Basic needs:** Strangely enough, in dealing with youngsters we sometimes forget the obvious truth that their basic human needs are the same as those of adults—such necessities as privacy, socialization, work, independence, and the opportunity to take **reasonable** risks. If we set limits at a place that prevents kids from meeting their basic needs, we can expect problems. For instance, if our limits for a 14 year old are so restrictive as not to allow her the opportunity to socialize with kids after school, we can expect one of two things to happen:

1. She will violate the limits, socialize with other kids, and our parental authority will be jeopardized.

2. Or she will abide by the limits, leaving our authority intact, but she'll miss out on achieving important developmental tasks that being with friends would provide.

So in failing to respect her needs we're encouraging either disobedience or immaturity. But showing respect for her basic needs helps her to respect herself—and kids who have healthy self-respect are less likely to get involved in alcohol or other drug problems.

Expect Kids to Test Limits

Sometimes we set limits at a place that seems so reasonable to us that we think our kids won't even be tempted to test them. Wrong. I've learned from long experience that no matter how reasonable a limit looks to parents, kids—especially adolescents—will try it, test it, push it. So expect it; it's part of their growing up; they learn by experience.

Fortunately, kids usually test limits by overstepping just one or two steps. If 10 o'clock is the limit, they'll probably try 10:30, say, but usually not 3 A.M. for starters. This gives us a clue. Try to set limits in such a way that if they do overstep them a bit, they won't be in deep trouble. To teach a two year old to look both ways before crossing the street, don't start out on a busy thoroughfare. Or if the police strictly enforce an 11 P.M. curfew, tell your kids to be home by 10:30.

When it comes to setting limits regarding alcohol and other drugs, though, allowing ANY use is too dangerous, as well as illegal; we must make it clear that we expect total abstinence. We might expect kids to test this limit, too, but if we allow any use at all our kids will believe we're condoning their use of alcohol and other drugs.

Do kids pay any real attention when parents discuss the dangers of alcohol and other drugs and make it clear that they're to avoid them completely? Surprisingly, the answer is **yes.** Research tells us that when kids make their decision about alcohol and other drugs, one of the most important factors in that decision is **what their parents think.** So don't give up just because kids keep testing limits you set. Kids do pay attention to what you're saying and doing; your patient efforts **will** pay off.

Enforce Limits

Once we've established clear, specific limits, we have to demonstrate that they mean something—that we're serious. This involves several points.

- We must **model** our respect for the limit if it's the sort of limit that should apply to us, too. If parents agree that we all should keep our feet off the furniture but Dad keeps putting his number twelves on the coffee table while watching TV, the kids aren't apt to take the rule very seriously either.

- We must **check** observance or nonobservance. If the video arcade is off limits but our kids know we never take the trouble to check compliance, we might as well forget the rule. Constant suspicion and constant checking into every last detail are quite a different matter. When our kids say they're going to practice after school for the class play, we need to have some idea of when practice starts and ends, and occasionally we need to check with the person in charge to see if they've attended. However, to call the teacher daily, to call our kids' friends to check, or to spy on their activities is going too far. It conveys a lack of trust that will eventually erode our relationship with our children.

- We must follow through with **definite consequences** when kids violate the limits. If Michael breaks his curfew, he must **know** that certain clear consequences will follow.

Setting Consequences

Perhaps no other item in our job description for parents fits in so clearly and powerfully with parents' overall goal of preparing their kids to deal with the real world as this one does. When parents prepare a reasonable, clear set of consequences that will predictably follow when kids act inappropriately, their kids can learn in a loving, supportive environment a lesson that the world outside often teaches in a harsh, unforgiving, even shattering, way—that actions have consequences. When kids who have learned at home that actions have consequences, they're more likely to consider what effects those decisions will have on themselves and on those they love.

What Nature and Society Teach Us About Consequences

The world teaches us the lesson about consequences day after day. Wise parents repeatedly point out this basic truth to their kids, both because it is a fundamental truth about the meaning of life and because it paves the way for parents to establish their own set of consequences that will reinforce what Nature and society are trying to tell us about our need to adjust to reality.

Nature continually teaches us that actions have consequences. With Nature, we need to remind ourselves and our kids that there are neither rewards nor punishments—only consequences. If we stand in the rain, we get wet. If we don't eat or sleep, we get sick. If we leap off a 20-story building onto a concrete pavement, we die.

Society also teaches that actions have consequences, even though society doesn't function nearly as inexorably or predictably as Nature does. Despite a lot of exceptions and mysterious variations, society does have its laws and customs, and persons who can't or won't observe them in a reasonable way tend to suffer the consequences. Drivers who run red lights do tend to get arrested and fined. People who cheat on taxes or who embezzle funds often wind up in prison. People who refuse to look for a job don't even make it to the bottom rung of the economic ladder. Kids who skip school or don't study get into trouble at school. In smaller, informal groups of friends or in private societies, people who won't act decently are ostracized and perhaps kicked out. The person who often drinks too much and insults people won't be tolerated for long. The individual who tells lies won't be trusted. The big kid who bullies the little kids on the block is thoroughly hated and avoided.

And so it goes: Both Nature and society teach us day after day that actions have consequences; that inappropriate behavior gets us in trouble. Parents need to point out that basic truth again and again to their children. Kids need to be told what will happen if they lick the frosted iron fence with their tongue, or if they sit for three hours clad only in their bathing suit the first time they go to the beach on a sweltering day in June. On the social level, parents need to remind kids that braggarts don't win any popularity contests, that shoplifters get picked up and saddled with a police record, that employees noted for laziness or incompetence or absenteeism are cellar dwellers in the big leagues of business, industry, and the professions.

It's clear, then, that parents must at all costs avoid the temptation to keep rescuing kids who **insist** on violating the laws of Nature or of society. The parent who hires an attorney to fight a speeding ticket that a youngster deserves, or who always takes the youngster's side against a teacher's reasonable demands, is sending exactly the wrong message: that actions **don't** have consequences; that it isn't important to accept responsibility for what one does. Kids who lack a sense of responsibility will be far more likely than others to give in to alcohol or other drugs.

Setting Up Effective Consequences

The guiding principle here is to **set up consequences that most effectively help our kids experience the full impact of their behavior.** Now, we should of course reward good behavior in such a way as to show that it brings pleasant consequences. Kids who prove they're trustworthy should be praised for it and allowed more free time and opportunity to exercise their growing sense of responsibility and judgment. That being said, and sincerely said, the fact is that most parents have a more difficult time knowing how to respond when kids have violated limits. So that will be our focus in this section.

Here are important qualities of effective consequences:

- **They're related to the incident:** "You didn't come home on time, so you're going to lose some free time."

- **They're reasonable:** "You were an hour late, so you'll lose two hours of your free time tomorrow night." It's reasonable that consequences usually exceed the violation; otherwise kids feel only a minimal impact. Speeding tickets usually cost adults considerably more time and money than they were hoping to save by driving beyond the speed limit.

- **They're timely:** The sooner the consequence follows the behavior, the more likely it is to be a learning experience. The 14-year-old boy who skips school on Thursday and has to stay home from a long-awaited Friday-night party experiences strong connections between actions and consequences.

- **They're not too elaborate:** It's a mistake to try to develop a system that covers every tiny bit of behavior and spells out an exact consequence for it. Such a complex system backfires because the child sees it as impossible to observe and will often end up blaming the parents even for failings that are clearly the child's own fault. Moreover, the system doesn't reflect the real world for which we're presumably preparing our child. In the real world it's not always perfectly clear what the exact results will be for every act of ours—not even for some of the more important ones, as a matter of fact. Many mobsters get wealthy and never spend a day in jail, and many well-respected persons are never unmasked as adulterers or child molesters. So when we develop an overly elaborate system of consequences, it teaches our kids the false message that the world will always respond to them in a prescribed, totally predictable way. Unfortunately, it also teaches them that the primary reason for being responsible is to avoid punishment. While it's important for kids to understand that consequences naturally follow behavior, it's equally important for them to begin developing a more mature level of morality. As kids mature they need to experience the internal satisfaction that goes hand in hand with being responsible.

- **They escalate in force:** One of the more important things youngsters must learn is that **patterns** of behavior are more important than isolated behaviors. Being late for a job once may result in little consequence for an adult; being late every other day for two weeks may result in very serious consequences. Consequences must increase in force for youngsters as well. A first-time tardiness may result in only a discussion with parents. But when it happens repeatedly, parents should increase the force of the consequences so that they have a greater impact. Let's say a 10 year old is told he must come home directly after school and do his chores before he goes out to play. The first time he neglects his responsibilities, we talk about how one earns privileges only by first taking care of responsibilities. The second time, he loses the privilege of going out to play the next afternoon. The third time, he loses the privilege for a week. The message registers that his parents mean business. Enjoying privileges means accepting responsibility.

As kids begin linking privileges with responsibility, they begin to associate responsibility with other more internal rewards such as pride, satisfaction, and being a contributing member of the family and of society. Kids who develop an internal set of reasons for being responsible are much less likely to become involved with alcohol or other drugs.

- **They're applied consistently:** No matter how good the system is in other respects, if parents don't apply it consistently, it fails. Being overly strict one day and overly permissive the next makes it impossible for kids to learn from their mistakes, because we establish no clear, predictable connection between their behavior and its consequences—the very opposite of what we want to teach them. Predictability and a feeling of security give way to confusion, insecurity, and resentment as kids are forced to play an endless, nerve-wracking game of Russian roulette.

- **They're enforced calmly, respectfully, without anger:** The spirit is "I'm sorry, but I'm sure you know it's the only thing we can do. You're a sweetheart and we love you, but you have to learn to take responsibility for what you do."

By now it should be clear how this whole practice of setting consequences is connected with the theme of this book: parenting that prevents our kids from ever getting involved with alcohol or other drugs. Kids whose parents have calmly, over many years, helped them to absorb and live by the basic truth that actions do have consequences will be in a stronger position when the time comes to make crucial decisions about using or not using alcohol or other drugs. They'll have developed the habit of thinking about the connection between behavior and its consequences, and so when they consider whether to use alcohol or other drugs they'll be realists. They'll see short-term consequences such as feeling guilty, getting caught by parents, school officials, or police, or being injured in a car accident. They'll see long-term consequences such as failing their studies, wrecking career plans, losing their good name, becoming alienated from family and friends, and eventually even losing their health and life itself. With such a background, their choices will be immeasurably easier to make.

What to Avoid in Setting Up Consequences

Experience and common sense have taught us some things to avoid in setting up consequences:

- **Seeking revenge:** It's easy to fool ourselves about our motives in setting up consequences. Instead of calmly and objectively looking at kids' inappropriate behavior and figuring out a reasonable way of educating them to take responsibility for it, we can easily focus on ourselves and take it personally. Angry and embarrassed, we sometimes settle for punishment that amounts to revenge. "He's not going to make fools of **us.** Let's give him a taste of his own medicine."

- **Punishing ourselves:** Some consequences are harder on the parents than on their children. Many couples I've worked with have delayed spending time alone together away from their kids for a number of years. When they finally do arrange for a weekend away, the children sometimes try to sabotage those plans by stealing out all night or coming home intoxicated. In this situation, setting consequences that don't interfere with the parents' plans require a fair amount of creativity. The adolescent might have to spend the weekend with a relative or in extreme cases even go to a detoxification center. Again, "grounding" sometimes hurts parents more than kids. Some kids are grounded for months at a time; some who come into treatment centers are grounded until the next decade. This type of consequence is often harder on us than on the child, because we're also grounding ourselves.

- **Rewarding inappropriate behavior:** Sometimes in our efforts to be fair and to find creative solutions, we actually reward our kid's inappropriate behavior. When we install our own private phone because the adolescent refuses to respect others' rights to the phone, we simply incur a bigger phone bill, and worse, we've rewarded selfishness by giving our youngster unrestricted phone privileges.

- **Making threats or promises:** Threats usually start with "If you don't stop that, I'm going to. . . ." Parents who are desperate because they can't control a child often resort to promises that amount to pleading: "If you'll just behave yourself tonight when the Balfes are here, I'll get you those designer jeans you've been asking for." Both methods usually fail because parents often don't follow through on them (especially on threats) and kids therefore learn not to take them seriously. Threats and promises not only have no educational value; they create uncertainty and even chaos. The child wonders **"Will** they follow through this time?" Parents wonder **"Should** we follow through?" As time goes on, the air in the home is thick with threats and promises that haven't been carried out but **might** be. Parents have vented their anger with threats, but have taken no action.

- **Shaming:** When kids **make** a mistake they feel guilt. When they feel they **are** a mistake they feel shame. We can shame our kids in many ways, but two of the most common occur when we

   1. fail to validate their needs as persons who need food, shelter, dignity, respect;

2. resort to using punishment that is dehumanizing (name-calling, physical abuse or threats of it, humiliation).

All children have a right to fulfillment of their basic human needs, both physical (food, shelter) and psychological (self-respect, love). To be deprived of these, or even to be threatened with such deprivation, is a degrading and shaming experience. Parents must never set consequences that deny or threaten such rights. Consequences such as name-calling, physical abuse or threats of it, or depriving a child of meals, shelter, dignity, or self-respect simply cannot be acceptable.

- **Overemphasizing consequences:** As we've indicated, setting reasonable consequences and discussing them with our children is a legitimate and important part of parenting. But it's only **one part** of parenting. If dealing with consequences becomes a primary parenting activity, if we become mere monitors of our children's behavior, it may be a signal of deeper family problems that we need to look into.

Creating Family Spirit and Building Structures

One of life's most beautiful experiences is to live in a close-knit family in which the members truly think and feel and act like a family. In such a family we sense a spirit of unity, togetherness. Each of the family members is loved and respected as a distinct, unique person, but at the same time there's a sense of common purpose and sharing as they all work out their destiny together.

In bygone ages, when society wasn't so complex and so hurried, it seemed a lot easier to build such a family. Today, many families have to try to cope with four or five different work schedules, numerous extracurricular activities, and loaded social calendars of parents and children alike. What we too often see, instead of a united family, is a group of individuals living in the same house but all pursuing their own private and isolated agendas.

Consider the Andersons. Jim and Sharon, the parents, both have full-time jobs and are also active in their church and in PTA; besides that, Jim belongs to the Rotary Club and likes to golf, and Sharon belongs to a bridge club and likes to bowl. To cap it off, Jim's company has just told him he'll have to travel out of town six or seven days a month. Meanwhile, Joan, age 14, and Jeffrey, age 11, both play in the band, participate in several sports, and lead an active social life after school and on many evenings.

Families like the Andersons (and many families with more complicated schedules) have little unity or togetherness; what they really know is fragmentation, loneliness, isolation. (I've known families who haven't eaten one meal together in months.) Lacking a family spirit of love and togetherness and mutual support, the kids look for it elsewhere, and far too often they find it in the fake good fellowship and high feelings they experience when they go along with the gang who's using alcohol or other drugs.

Is it possible, in such a society as ours, to build a close-knit, united, loving family where kids can grow into healthy, happy adults who've never been seduced into resorting to alcohol or other drugs? **Definitely yes.** Here are two reasons why.

First, the gloomy portrait of a whole society whose families are fragmented and chaotic is a gross exaggeration. Despite our many problems and hectic schedules, most parents really are concerned about their kids and are already doing a lot of things right—and the fact that you're reading this book probably means you're among them.

The second reason I'm confident we can build close-knit, united, loving families is that in dealing with hundreds of such families I've learned a **number of specific techniques** they've used to get where they are today. Here are a few of them. If you'll study them, think them over, adopt them but adapt them sensibly to your own situation, I know they'll work for you, too.

- **Family schedules:** Set up a weekly calendar outlining where everyone is and when they'll be home, with family activities and events highlighted.

- **Family activities:** Schedule daily or weekly family activities that occur regularly and that all family members are expected to attend—for example, weekly worship.

- **Family events:** Plan special activities such as a visit to the zoo, amusement park, or nursing home; outings, vacations.

- **Family meetings:** Hold weekly meetings to air feelings or concerns, review events, activities, and schedules of family members. Time is set aside to discuss both problems and successes.

- **House-utilization plan:** Make up a schedule for high-use areas of the house, such as bathrooms in the morning, family room in the evening, laundry room on Saturday.

These plans spell out both when such areas of the house are to be used and any special rules governing those areas. Oftentimes kids can contribute nicely to these plans at the weekly meeting.

- **House/yard-work schedule:** Line up duties and make it clear that everyone in the family is expected to do certain daily chores without expecting remuneration. Kids learn to contribute to the larger society by contributing at home. To understand the importance of giving, kids must experience it first in their own family.

Family practices like these help counter the chaos that does characterize some families today. They give our families reasonable structure, regularity, and order without turning them into rigid military units. Ultimately, by bringing the family together frequently in a relaxed, pleasant atmosphere they help us create a true family spirit: a spirit of togetherness, mutual respect, sharing, and love that lessens the probability that kids will turn to alcohol or other drugs.

Handling Our Own Mistakes and Problems

An important duty of parents is that of presenting a human image to the children. Like all other mortals, parents make mistakes and have to face problems. Handling those mistakes and problems sensibly is important, because how we do it has profound effects on our kids. Here are some down-to-earth recommendations. We need to:

- **Admit our mistakes:** For some reason, we expect godlike perfection of ourselves, so we try to hide our mistakes from our kids. This puts enormous pressure on us, encourages us to be phony, and teaches our kids that making and admitting mistakes is something shameful. That, in turn, puts unrealistic, unnecessary pressure on **them** to aim at impossible perfection and, when they fail, to cover up.

- **Admit our problems:** Sometimes we even go so far as to deny that we have problems. Perhaps we do it to shelter our kids from the harsh realities of the real world. But it won't work. Kids usually see through us anyway, and they suffer more stress from knowing we're hiding problems from them than if we openly admitted them. Even if they don't fully realize our cover-up, though, they sense that something is wrong, and when we deny the problem, they begin to distrust their own ability to discover what's real.

- **Avoid blaming our kids for our mistakes or problems:** Since our kids, especially younger ones, tend to think of us as perfect, they quite naturally figure it must be **their** fault when things go wrong in the family. But if we blame them for our mistakes or problems, we of course double their stress.

- **Be willing to get help:** No matter what the problem is—alcoholism, marital stress, difficulty with mental or physical health, finances—**help is available.** We can explain to Billy that Mom and Dad are seeing a counselor to help sort out their disagreements. Counselors, we tell him, are nothing more than people who help us see why we're disagreeing and how we can better understand each other's point of view. Our counselor, we explain, has helped us discover better ways to talk with each other without losing our tempers. It's important for kids to realize it's normal to reach out for help in times of need.

In short, when we handle our own mistakes and problems honestly and calmly, we're teaching our kids a great deal about how to face the realities of everyday life. They need such role models. When they make their own mistakes and get into their own difficulties, they'll have healthy attitudes, and they'll also know they can come to us for understanding and practical help.

Team Parenting

Team parenting is one of the best insurance policies against our kids' use of alcohol and other drugs. But it's often difficult to achieve because "opposites attract," as the old saying reminds us. Sometimes it's almost as though we select our spouse to complement our own strengths and weaknesses but then spend a fair amount of our lives refusing to cooperate with him or her. It's not uncommon for a parent who believes in strict discipline to find that the other tends to be quite lenient. Marriages that reflect such totally opposite approaches often get into trouble and end in divorce. But opposite styles can be incorporated into a unified approach if parents learn to work as a team. In fact, the strongest teams are made up of couples who bring together a diversity of perspectives and skills. However, spouses have to get rid of faulty ideas that undermine team parenting. Here are some of them.

Faulty Ideas About Team Parenting

- **"I'll parent them when they're good; you parent them when they're bad."** The problem with this is that one parent is the good guy and the other is the bad guy. Mom, let's say, deals with the kids when things go along smoothly, but if they get out of hand it's "Wait till I tell your father when he comes home." So Mom is the sweet Rewarder and Dad is the villainous Enforcer. You can do what you want when Mom's around, but you can't call your life your own when Dad's here.

  This setup creates problems for both parents. To get out of the pattern, Mom needs to begin setting consequences on her own. While it might be easier to ignore things till Dad gets back, to do so only prolongs the problem. On the other hand, Dad will have to establish other bases for his relationship with his kids. He needs to learn to be reassuring, fun, and more easy-going. That can be difficult when he's been identified mostly as the Enforcer, but it's a way out of that trap.

- **"I'll parent the boys; you parent the girls."** Some couples believe that boys need fathers to set limits for them, and girls need mothers to set limits for them. The unspoken assumption behind this view seems to be that women are by nature loving and nurturing, but weak, and that men are by nature strong but harsh, so children can learn only from the respective parent how to be a **real** woman or a **real** man. Fortunately, these stereotypes that have little basis in reality are disappearing in our time as we learn that women can and should be strong and men can and should be loving and nurturing. But the stereotypes are by no means dead, so we need to abandon exclusive same sex parenting and allow both the parents and the children to become whole persons. For instance, it's important for moms to be active and interested in Scouting programs, athletics, and other activities previously considered men's activities. It's equally important for dads to be involved with clothes shopping, school conferences, and parenting classes, which often seem to attract mostly moms.

- **"I'll parent them when they're babies, you parent them when they're in grade school, and we'll both quit parenting when they're teenagers."** Many parents prefer to deal with kids at one particular stage of their development. But they need us at every stage. It's important for us to go through each of these stages with them, to share their good times and their bad times. Avoiding a kid during a particular stage can be a reflection of our own unmet needs as children at that age. The desire to avoid our child's behavior should be discussed with a counselor. Understanding our own unmet needs can keep us from depriving our children of what they need from us.

Four Tips About Team Parenting

- **Kids need consistency:** Even though our parenting styles can be polar opposites, we simply have to reach a workable agreement on the basics of limits, consequences, and family spirit and structures. Otherwise it's chaos. Some families follow one set of rules when Dad's at home and another when he's on the road. So the kids view Dad as the heavy disciplinarian and Mom as a pushover, even though neither parent wants it that way. Becoming consistent takes work. It's important to sit down with our spouse, take out a paper and pencil, and list areas where we've noticed differences in how we handle things. Then we can discuss how those differences are affecting us and the kids. Some differences are nothing more than stylistic issues that really cause no one any harm. Other differences can be much more substantial and cause continual parental struggles. For instance, if one parent feels comfortable and confident enforcing curfews and the other parent prefers to ignore the violations of curfew, this can become a serious issue. To avoid resolving such a difference will make kids feel uncertain and therefore insecure.

If you and your spouse find that problems with consistency continue to plague your parenting, it may signal other underlying problems. If so, it's important to seek outside counseling as a couple. To neglect resolving these underlying issues leaves your kids trapped in marital dynamics that can be debilitating for them. My clinical experience indicates that kids who get trapped in these adult marital disagreements end up taking on stress that they can do nothing about and that they're significantly more vulnerable to using alcohol or other drugs to relieve that stress.

• **Parents can learn from each other:** Perhaps the reason why opposites attract is that the fusion gives balance and complementary strengths. One parent may be highly organized and therefore loves to plan things thoroughly, down to the last detail of written lists. The other may be spontaneous and therefore loves to do things on the spur of the moment. It's good to expose kids to both these approaches to structure and planning, provided we don't spend our time and energy disagreeing. If we reach a sensible accommodation that capitalizes on the strengths of both approaches, we demonstrate to our kids the beauty of diversity, and they begin to absorb life skills relating to compromise, cooperation, and appreciating differences in people.

- **Strategize away from the kids:** Professional parents (such as foster parents or group-home parents) make it a practice to get away from their kids regularly to meet with a clinical supervisor who gives them expert help on parenting. It's important that ordinary parents also get away at times so they can work out a consistent parenting approach, especially to discuss volatile issues that arouse strong emotions—emotions that might get out of hand if the kids were around. (Parents who feel, for example, that their kids are deliberately playing them against each other or against the school system often get so angry they want to lash out at the kids in the heat of anger.) If an objective third party, such as a counselor, school professional, or trusted friend is available, so much the better. Seminars and parent-education classes can also give parents new ideas about working together.

- **Getting support as a single parent:** Being a single parent can be difficult, but also has its payoffs. As one single parent said, "At least I don't have to argue with someone about what the consequences for misbehavior will be." One of the more challenging difficulties in being a single parent happens when our ex-spouse maintains a very different set of standards and expectations for the kids. Consistently, the kids will compare one household with the other and attempt to pit one parent against the other in an attempt to bargain for more permissive limits. Strong-willed children in particular have the ability to take full advantage of the situation. Unfortunately, in winning, they actually lose. As they break their parents down, they inevitably get more power and independence than they can handle and frequently get into trouble.

The best way to prevent the triangular pattern of kids playing off divorced parents is to establish a baseline of communication regarding limits and expectations in each household. While it can be difficult to set aside past resentments to resolve such matters, the time and effort is well spent. If negotiations with an ex-spouse are impossible, the best alternative is to explain to the kids that this house is run differently than their other house. When they are in this home, the limits and expectations will be consistently enforced. Comparisons between the two households should be ignored. (Some kids actually bring up comparisons between households simply to get a reaction from their parents.)

Providing a Safe Home Environment

A safe home environment is one where the kids feel emotionally secure and physically safe. This environment provides for the daily needs of the individual: adequate sleep, food, shelter, privacy, dignity and respect, order, structure, and stability. In a safe environment these basic needs are never questioned or never taken away as a consequence, no matter what the behavior.

Whenever these basic necessities are taken away or threatened, most of us experience extreme insecurity, especially when we feel powerless to control the situation. We must remember that our kids live in an environment where they're never in charge, where they're habitually vulnerable because we're their parents. Because our kids are vulnerable, both they and our society interpret any violation of their basic needs as abuse.

Kinds of Abuse

Three types of abuse occur in our homes more frequently than most of us like to admit. Exposure to any of these abuse patterns will multiply a child's chances of developing alcohol or other drug problems, for reasons we'll mention in a moment.

- **Emotional abuse:** Neglect, abandonment, humiliation, shame, and being made to feel unneeded, unwanted, or unimportant do untold damage to a child's self-esteem. For instance, when we're angry with our kids for violating limits in a way that makes us feel personally attacked or offended, it's easy to lash out at them in ways that make them feel unwanted. "I wish I'd never had you," "Life would be so much easier without you," or "I wish you'd just go away" can sometimes roll out of our mouths without our comprehending the impact it may have on our kids. We know we love our kids, and so we assume they'll interpret our behavior in light of that overarching truth. But kids often can't distinguish how we feel about a situation from how we really feel about them. So we must be very conscious of the messages we give them. When we're confronting them on negative behavior we must be sure they realize the confrontation is about their **behavior,** not about **them.** Our kids must realize that they make mistakes and will be called on them. However, they must never be made to feel that **they** are a mistake, that they're bad persons because they make mistakes. (Chapter 11 gives a specific technique for confronting kids' behavior versus attacking their personhood.)

Some other ways in which kids are often abused emotionally are name-calling, not acknowledging their needs, or enforcing inappropriate discipline, often because we interpret misbehavior as a personal affront to us. We can be especially vulnerable to personalizing our kids' behavior when their actions directly affect us. For example, when an adolescent uses our car without permission and has an accident with it, this behavior infuriates us not only because it violates limits we've set but because it damages our property, creates inconvenience, and costs us a lot of money.

- **Physical abuse:** Technically, physical abuse occurs whenever a child is physically damaged by interaction with an adult. Although it's legal to use corporal punishment such as spanking, it isn't an effective or healthy way to enforce limits or teach self-discipline. Any type of corporal punishment is especially damaging to kids in their late childhood or adolescence. It runs the double risk of crossing the line into physical abuse and of humiliating someone whose sense of self-esteem is already very fragile. This type of punishment often leads to escalating power conflicts between the child and parent, teaches the child fear and mistrust, is very demeaning, and diminishes self-esteem and self-respect.

- **Sexual abuse:** Sexual abuse occurs when family members or adults indulge in any type of sexual activity or seductive or suggestive behavior with a young person. As we become more willing to accept testimony about sexual abuse, it's shocking to realize the number of families experiencing this problem. While the perpetrators in these situations are usually men, the victims aren't always females. An increasing number of young boys are being reported as sexual abuse victims, often as victims of an adult family member.

Family members often intuitively sense what's going on even when any kind of abusive behavior is kept secret. It's important for family members to take any suspected abuse seriously, because it's too prevalent and damaging to ignore. Bringing the abusive behavior out into the open and recognizing it as destructive behavior is the indispensable first step in helping the victim as well as the rest of the family.

When young people report abuse—physical, emotional, or sexual—they're usually telling the truth. Help is available and accessible. If you suspect or know that abuse is occurring in your family, you can get immediate help by looking under Child Abuse Services in the yellow pages of your local telephone directory or by contacting:

- National Committee to Prevent Child Abuse
  332 South Michigan Ave., Suite 950
  Chicago, Illinois 60604
  (312) 663-3520

- Local police

- Local county mental health or social service agency

- Local Parents' Anonymous Intergroup

The research clearly indicates that kids who have been victimized physically, sexually, or emotionally are significantly more likely to use alcohol and other drugs. The feelings of shame, fear, and rage that result from abuse often lead the young person to use alcohol or other drugs as a way of escaping those uncomfortable emotions.

Summary

This job description for parents has given you a set of guidelines and a brief discussion of your main duties as parents, with a view to helping you prevent your children from getting involved with alcohol or other drugs. If you faithfully follow these guidelines, you'll be doing your part in establishing a whole family atmosphere in which your kids can develop the indispensable life skills we'll cover in Part 2— skills that will make it immeasurably easy for your kids to say no to alcohol and other drugs.

In our next chapter we'll discuss a job description for kids—things they're responsible for if they're to grow up as balanced, happy persons. Inseparably intertwined with their responsibilities, though (as we'll see further), is parents' continuing, difficult task of "letting go."

5

A Job Description for Kids

Sometimes it's easy to give a job description if we look at someone who's not doing that job well. Consider Jennifer. Her mom, who's a single parent,

- wakes her up morning after morning because she often oversleeps
- drives her to school because she's often late or skips
- does her laundry for her because she refuses to do her own
- cleans her room because otherwise it would be an absolute mess
- nags her continually about doing her homework and often gives her answers to problems she won't tackle
- doesn't require her to earn some of her spending money by having a part-time job
- always gives in at the first sign of her crying or outburst.

Let's look back after several years of such parenting and see what happened to Jennifer. Overall, she quickly learned that it was easy to avoid her responsibilities, because her mom would take over her duties and would bail her out of any trouble she got into. She became lazy, careless, inconsiderate of others.

The more her mom took over for her, the more dependent she became, but at the same time she'd lash out at her with anger and resentment. Her self-image was in the gutter, but she covered her real feelings with a rigid defense system: It was really all her mother's fault; besides, things weren't so bad—her mom just liked to make a big deal out of nothing.

What happened next wasn't surprising. When her friends offered her alcohol and other drugs, she easily gave in. Alcohol and other drugs made her forget her troubles, made her feel good. Pretty soon they were a way of life—she was hooked.

The next step for Jennifer was treatment for chemical dependence. That's when her mom finally came to realize what had happened. When Jennifer was just a little girl, she'd had a long bout with asthma, and her concerned parents had gotten into the habit of doing **everything** for her. But when the asthma cleared up, they went right on babying her—with the results we've just seen. During and after the divorce, her mother, who had to fight for custody, actually became more overprotective. Their counselor now pointed out two closely intertwined things that had happened.

First, the parents' concern and overprotectiveness went right on even after the asthma was no longer a problem. To them, she was still the helpless, lovable little child even as she reached adolescence and wanted a legitimate measure of independence. The difficult feelings that everyone went through during the divorce only reinforced the mom's feelings of having to protect Jennifer. In short, **Jennifer's mother didn't know how to let go.** Second, by taking over Jennifer's responsibilities, **she in effect taught her to be irresponsible;** she refused to let her grow up, to develop the skills she needed to face the world as a healthy, independent young adult. One of the sad results was Jennifer's inability to say no to alcohol and other drugs.

A Time-Tested Job Description for Kids

Jennifer and her mom might have been spared an immense amount of suffering if she had formulated and implemented a clear job description for kids. I offer such a description here— one based not only on my own experience but on that of hundreds of parents, kids, and well-informed family counselors. This sensible description of kids' major responsibilities is really aimed both at parents and at kids. Since parents are the family leaders, they must know what to expect of their kids, and kids need to know what's expected of them. Families that follow this job description engage in a twofold, simultaneous process. Kids learn how to accept responsibility for their lives, and parents learn how to let go—which means not only **allowing** their kids to experience a growing measure of freedom but also **encouraging** them to do so. Freedom and responsibility go together. Handled with good sense, they spell maturity, the ability to deal with the real world. And that's what all good parents want their kids to achieve.

Here, then, are the major areas for which kids are responsible:

- their feelings
- their behavior

- their school performance
- their social life
- consequences from outside the home
- their future.

Feelings

One of the primary reasons kids use alcohol and other drugs is that they expect these substances to help them manage, control, or numb their feelings. It's important that we help our children to deal with their feelings, especially the uncomfortable ones. We need to explain the simple truth that feelings need to be talked through because others can't read our minds. We can serve as sounding boards for our kids by listening and then helping them identify, own, and express their feelings appropriately. Specific tools for helping kids learn to deal with their feelings will be discussed in Chapter 6.

We sometimes get hooked into taking responsibility for our kids' feelings. Here are some of the ways:

- **Giving in to their outbursts of emotion:** For example, when our kids want us to let them go to the dance even though they've been restricted that evening for coming in late the night before, we can expect a show of emotions. Some kids will cry, some will pout, others will stamp their feet and display anger. While this may seem to be only an expression of feelings, it is, in fact, an attempt to get us to take responsibility for their feelings. ("**You're** the reason I feel so bad. If you'd just let me go to the dance, everything would be all right.") But if we give them the message that the world will change because of how they feel, we encourage them to use their feelings to manipulate people.

- **Habitually rescuing them from situations that cause them to feel rejection, loneliness, or pain:** When adolescents come home describing how they feel because a friend has abandoned them for someone else, we must of course be sympathetic and understanding. But we must be careful not to **interfere** in those peer relationships. Our kids need to learn that relationships are necessarily filled with intense positive and negative feelings, so when we enter into relationships we must be prepared for both the good and the bad. If we always protect our kids from these negative feelings, we're in effect telling them they're so fragile they must rely on others for protection and intervention. But by allowing them to work through these feelings, we help them to learn the nature of relationships and the importance of choosing friends wisely.

Kids need to learn to look at their feelings as friends. The world won't change just because they have feelings. Like thermometers, feelings tell us our emotional temperature; like barometers, they let us know if a storm is brewing. They tell us, for instance, who or what we're attracted to, what we fear or dislike. They tell us what we need to do, and they often provide the impetus or energy for doing it.

Behavior

One of the false ideas we often accept is that we can or should be able to **control** our kids' behavior. It's one thing to establish limits for our children, but only they themselves can assume responsibility for their behavior. Some ways we mistakenly assume responsibility for our kids' behavior are:

- blaming ourselves, our spouse, or the school when our kids misbehave
- forcing our kids to do things our way because we know better
- not allowing our kids to make mistakes or fail.

Kids must learn from experience that they can and will survive mistakes and failures and that it's their willingness to keep on trying that really counts. If we prevent them from taking risks or from failing, they'll never develop a capacity for constructive, creative risk-taking, and that can harmfully affect their level of achievement throughout their lives. For example, people never learn how to speak in front of an audience unless they take that first step and risk looking foolish. Only by going out on a limb and trying something they can hardly imagine themselves doing will they ever learn their potential or have the courage to accept new challenges.

School Performance

It's perfectly acceptable for parents to set a limit that says all their school-age children will spend a certain amount of time each night studying quietly with no TV or radio. The specific study time requirement will vary with the child's age. A good rule is: ages 7-9, 15-20 minutes; 10-12, 30-45 minutes; 14-18, 1-2 hours. While it's our right and responsibility to enforce study times, it's quite another thing to take responsibility for the outcome of the studying. Kids must always feel that their school performance is a direct result of their own efforts.

School gives many kids their first challenge to live up to certain performance standards set by someone outside the family circle. Now, it's true that school performance often indicates a child's future success or failure and that parents should work closely and cooperatively with the school. But if we concentrate too much on kids' meeting rigid and rather narrow performance standards such as grades, we might well encourage them to miss the whole, deeper meaning of education and to end up hating school.

For example, we take on too much responsibility for school performance when we become more interested in the outward signs of school performance than in what the educational experience is doing for our child's sense of self—for example, when we become highly concerned with their

- achieving a specific grade point
- getting the scholarship
- winning the award
- making the team or being a cheerleader
- being the homecoming queen, king, class president, or captain of the debate team.

Here are some ways we can really help our kids:

- Show approval for their efforts and self-discipline rather than the outward signs of success.

- Work on developing their individual talents and abilities and motivating them to do their best for their own sake.

- Work on our personal relationships with them by spending at the very least an hour per week talking about their activities and concerns.

- Allow them opportunities for personal growth and social development by encouraging them to invite friends to the house and to be active in extracurricular events and leisure-time activities.

Kids whose parents become overly invested in their school performance often either rebel or else accept the pressure of their parents' expectations and become vulnerable to quick and easy solutions for relief such as cheating on tests, overeating, withdrawing, or resorting to alcohol or other drug use.

Social Life

It's our responsibility to set limits concerning the social life of our kids. For example:

- "You must be in by 11 P.M."
- "You may not date anyone more than two years older than you."
- "People who pick you up in cars must be people we know or who come in and meet us."
- "If you go to parties, we must know at whose home the party will be held and who'll chaperone; and there can't be any alcohol or other drugs."

Such limits don't interfere with our kids' capacity to select friends and deepen relationships with them—a huge issue for adolescents, because at that stage they're beginning to transfer to the peer group some of the bonds they've built with their family.

But kids correspondingly need to learn that (as elsewhere) consequences will inevitably follow their choices and that they must take responsibility for their choice of friends. Some of those consequences might well lead them into activities that can affect their reputation, even their legal record and their career. If Marge's friend Debbie is caught shoplifting while Marge is with her, friends and police alike might well be suspicious of Marge. Whether our kids choose friends who use alcohol and other drugs or who engage in vandalism or other illegal behavior is ultimately up to them. But we need to point out to them that our free choice of friends **does** tell a great deal about who we really are. Whatever choices we make, then, we must take responsibility for them and be ready to accept the consequences.

If we believe our kids when they defend their poor choices with excuses such as "Everybody uses alcohol and other drugs" or "Everyone I know shoplifts once in a while" or "Everybody at our school goes to keggers," we're enabling (encouraging) their poor choice of friends. The reality is that many adolescents are leading positive, responsible lives, and that our own children can find such friends.

In short, while our kids should be free to choose friends with whom they'll feel comfortable, they must learn to accept responsibility for their choices and for any ensuing consequences. For instance, Scott may choose to be friends with Bob, but Scott **still** must be home at 9 even though Bob's parents allow him to be out till 10:30. If Scott continues to violate curfew as a result of being with Bob, he must be prepared to face the escalating consequences. We should never compromise our limits to accommodate the standards of others.

Consequences from Outside the Home

Here we're referring to consequences that flow from our kids' choices of behavior, without any action of ours. These can often educate our kids in ways that consequences we set up could never provide. It's essential, of course, that we do set up consequences; but oddly enough, the very fact that our kids know we love them often makes them suspicious. For example, when we take away free time because kids come in late, they often don't believe that anything like that will happen in the "real" world. They think that what we're doing is merely a contrived, artificial teaching device. They're far more likely to accept consequences such as speeding tickets, suspension or expulsion from school or from athletic teams as real lessons about how the world works, because they know that such consequences are more or less automatic and happen to people irrespective of their status or their relationships with others.

Despite the obvious value of consequences initiated from outside the home, some parents insist on interfering with them. For example, we:

- get our child off the legal hook by paying the fine for illegal parking
- hire a top-notch attorney to help our child avoid the consequences of a serious legal violation such as a DWI, stealing, vandalism, or breaking and entering
- use our influence with school officials to soften the consequences of an athletic-code violation such as smoking pot or drinking
- believe our kids when they tell us that the police, school, and legal systems are just hassling them because those systems really have nothing better to do than to set traps for them.

Sometimes our kids really may be subjected to unfair consequences from the outside. But unless we have solid evidence to the contrary, interfering with those outside consequences will usually teach our kids that there's always someone who will bail them out of tough situations. Letting them deal with those consequences on their own will teach them that even if the world is sometimes unfair, they can stand up for themselves and defend their positions. This is a message our young people need to learn if they're to develop the maturity, self-respect, and integrity that make adulthood meaningful and fulfilling.

Future

We all worry about what our kids will be when they grow up. Since most of us think we know a lot about what the real world has to offer, it's tempting to fall into the trap of trying to control the decisions they must ultimately make regarding their future. Some of the methods we use are:

- **Demanding that they attend a specific college to meet the "right" people:** "We won't pay for your college education unless you attend Princeton. Otherwise you're on your own."

- **Expecting them to have long-term plans at too early an age:** "What do you mean, you don't know what you want to be? You're going to be a senior next year, and colleges are already accepting applications from your classmates. If you don't decide now, you're always going to be a day late and a dollar short." (Actually, most kids don't have a clear idea of their career plans until their early to mid-twenties.)

- **Expecting them to measure up to adult standards of understanding and being motivated by far distant consequences:** "It's important to do well now that you're in ninth grade. Your high school grade point average will be critical in your getting accepted into the private college that your mom and I've been planning for you to attend." Kids think they'll live forever (so there's no hurry) and that they're immune to possible later consequences.

- **Expecting them to choose a specific vocation, job, or career that we'd prefer:** "Don't you think it'd be wonderful if you'd become a successful lawyer like your Uncle Bob?"

Testing Ourselves on Letting Go

When we get to know a young person who has fallen victim to alcohol or other drug abuse or addiction, we usually find a young adult (and it can be equally true of a chronologically middle-aged adult) who is still excessively attached to and dependent on his or her family. By learning to let go of our children constructively, we're not only helping them to mature into responsible adults; we're also actively discouraging their involvement with alcohol or other drugs. By contrast, I know a 29-year-old man who suffers from alcohol and other drug addiction and who continues to move around the country from family member to family member, refusing to accept the responsibilities of adulthood. After encouraging his irresponsibility for years, his family has finally participated in various therapy and treatment programs, and family members are now beginning to understand the importance of letting go. As long as those who are close to addicts continue to rescue them from consequences directly related to their alcohol or other drug problem, the addiction **will** go on.

The following exercise will help us to begin seeing some specific areas where we can get hooked (or already have been hooked) into taking on too much responsibility for our kids.

A Self-Test on Letting Go

1. Check any of the following areas where you honestly think you take on too much responsibility for your child's behavior (that is, areas where you fail to let go).

____ Athletic performance	____ Feeling of hurt
____ Grades	and rejection
____ Extracurricular activities	____ Anger
____ Choice of friends	____ Decision making
____ Popularity	____ Legal problems
____ Success in dating	____ School consequences
____ College plans	(such as detention or
____ Career choices and plans	suspension)
____ Disappointments	____ Job

2. After completing the checklist, look at each area and either keep a journal or, better, discuss with your spouse or someone who knows you as a parent, your fears or worries about what would happen if you were to let go in areas you checked. For each area consider both a worst-case and a best-case scenario of what might happen if you were to let go in that area.

    For instance, suppose your son has felt hurt and disappointed upon learning he's not in the same first grade class with many of his best friends. You might write in your journal, "I have a difficult time letting go of my son's feelings of hurt and disappointment, because I want him always to be happy." Then you write this worst-case/best-case scenario about letting go by not calling the school to have him switched to a different class. "Worst case: my son might continue to feel hurt and disappointed, and those feelings might turn him completely against school. Best case: adjusting to new friends might help him develop social skills that will broaden him as a person. As I look at both scenarios, it's clear to me that it's much better to let go—I won't involve myself in this situation at all."

Many parents who do this exercise find that most of their worst fears are irrational. Often in doing the second part of the exercise they discover that even if they're still convinced that their fears and worries are rational and legitimate, they become more aware that as parents they can do very little about them anyway. As a result, the exercise really does help them to let go.

Letting Go as a Grieving Process

As I pointed out earlier, the helpless infant who depends on us for practically everything gradually outgrows that total dependence. For us, it's a bittersweet experience to rejoice in our child's development but also to realize that he or she needs us less and less and in fact begins to question and even reject our guidance.

Adolescence especially is a time when our youngster questions our values and the limits we set and may even rebel outright. Unless we have a clear-headed view of this natural process by which our kids move toward independence in a life apart from us, we can misunderstand it as a personal rejection. It's a time when many parents react by trying to use excessive control over their kids—which amounts really to taking on the kids' responsibilities. As parents continue to take on those responsibilities, they're sheltering the kids from the consequences of their behavior. The kids become more and more irresponsible and may even fall into self-destructive behavior such as alcohol or other drug abuse.

The process of "letting go" of our children is difficult at best, but it helps if we realize that what we go through is actually a grief process—the kind of experience we have when someone we love dies or goes out of our life in some other way. Let's look at the case of Tom and his father.

Tom's dad, an attorney, hoped Tom would follow in his footsteps. Early on, Tom seemed interested. He was involved in such activities as debate, and he joined the school's legal club. During eleventh grade, though, he dropped out of the debate team so he'd have more time with the rock group he'd been playing with.

His father had a difficult time allowing Tom to make this decision, because it seemed as if Tom were breaking off his whole relationship with his dad. For his dad this was an experience laden with grief.

In working with parents faced with similar letting-go situations, I've noticed that the process follows the five stages of grief as described in Elisabeth Kübler-Ross's work: denial, anger/guilt, bargaining, depression, and acceptance. The following paragraphs apply these stages to the loss parents feel during the letting-go phase of parenting.

- **Denial Stage:** Initially we simply deny that the loss has occurred. One common way to recognize that we're in this stage is by finding ourselves thinking or saying things like "I can't believe how my little baby has grown" or "He (she) can't be doing that already; he (she) is only a kid." The denial stage insulates us from the many feelings we associate with loss and grief. As we begin to accept the reality that we indeed are losing our child, various feelings usually come rushing to the surface, especially anger and guilt, the second stage.

- **Anger/Guilt Stage:** Feelings of anger are a natural initial emotional response to any loss. Many parents turn their anger inward, and then the emotion shifts from anger to guilt. (Many professionals who work with emotions recognize that guilt is sometimes nothing more than anger turned inward.) For instance, when Tom first dropped out of debate his dad was enraged. As time went on, his anger eventually shifted to guilt as he wondered if he'd been pushing Tom too hard in only one direction. Some of the things we say to ourselves as we feel this anger/guilt are:

He (she) wouldn't be doing this if:

- I were home more
- we didn't live in this neighborhood
- he (she) had different friends
- we hadn't divorced
- we had divorced
- he (she) really loved us.

Anger/guilt is a normal part of letting go of someone we love. The more we're attached to someone, the more intense the feelings, and there's probably no one we love more than our kids. In the process of dealing with these emotions, it's essential that we have some **constructive outlet for talking**

these things out. Talking with friends, our spouse, our pastor, or counselor really does help neutralize the feelings. Our feelings of guilt can drive us crazy if we try to bear them alone, and they can be one of the primary obstacles in learning to let go of our children in a constructive way.

- **Bargaining Stage:** In trying to neutralize these difficult and gnawing feelings of anger and guilt, we often go to this third stage: bargaining with our kids. We try to 1) bribe them into being the kind of young adult we had hoped they'd be or 2) keep them dependent on us financially and/or emotionally. Or 3) we resort to a tactic completely opposite to bribery: We try to get them totally out of our house and out of our sight so that we won't have to acknowledge any of the difficult feelings associated with letting go. This third tactic is sometimes referred to as the ejection-seat process. It's common in families with alcohol or other drug-abuse problems. In an unconscious reaction to this process, five adolescents of one family I worked with all created various types of crises such as teen pregnancy, suicide attempts, and alcohol and other drug abuse in order to eject themselves from the family. As a result, neither parents nor children had to deal with feelings associated with leaving home or breaking family ties.

Parents can find it especially difficult to let go of a youngest child or of one who is special (for example, one with a disability such as asthma, diabetes, or mental retardation).

As we finally accept the initial emotions and reality of our loss, it's not unusual to sink into the fourth stage, depression.

- **Depression Stage:** When we face the fact that our kids are really going to leave, depression often sets in. The years of parenting are over, we realize, and the longer we've been parents, the deeper this depression can be. The sadness of the loss becomes very strong. Some of us become immobilized; others of us turn inward and become bitter. The key to our ability to move on consists usually of discovering new activities, finding new friends, and beginning to plan the next stage of our lives. The darkness of the depression begins to lift as we rediscover many things about life that were rewarding before children entered the scene and as we discover new interests and new talents.

- **Acceptance Stage:** Acceptance happens only when we both acknowledge and bow to the reality of our kids' independence and when we resolve the feelings associated with that reality. Our love for our children doesn't end or even diminish. Instead, we redirect it in a way that allows our kids to become adults. This stage usually marks the beginning of a new "peer relationship" with our children. As they establish themselves as adults, they return to visit with us, but the basis of the relationship is different. Most parents say they're surprised at the depth of joy they discover in this new relationship with their children. "I never thought my relationship with my son/daughter could be so beautiful" is a typical response.

Acceptance of our kids as adults allows us to participate with them in the adult stages of their life. We and they will share such adult experiences of their lives as marriage and child-rearing: we as loving but healthily disengaged parents— they as adult children. But if we avoid these processes of letting go, we'll continue to undermine our children's attempts at being successful, fulfilled, responsible adults.

Summary

Kids must learn to be responsible for themselves. Many of the parents I've worked with have an easier time with accepting responsibility than they do with letting go of it. The hard reality for us to accept as parents is that if we take on responsibilities which in fact are our kids', we actually undermine their developing sense of responsibility and maturity. As painful as it can be, we must allow our kids to become responsible, even if they sometimes stumble along the way. Interfering with this developing sense of responsibility creates a handicap or weakness that makes them easy targets for alcohol or other drugs.

As we go on now to Part 2, we'll build on the foundations we've laid in Part 1. We'll further explore practical strategies and techniques that will help us to help our kids learn the life skills they'll need to say no to alcohol and other drugs. In a culture such as ours, where alcohol and other drug abuse is so common, they'll be called on to use those skills day in and day out.

PART 2

Teaching Life Skills to Our Kids

Introduction to Part 2

In Part 1 we laid the foundations of parenting for prevention. Part 2 explains the life skills that kids **must** have if they're to resist alcohol and other drugs. Before we discuss those skills one by one, though, we need to mention two points: the huge changes that have swept through our culture in recent years, and some basic terms we'll use in discussing how to teach life skills.

Our Changed and Changing Culture

We've always learned life skills from our families, within our homes. But in relatively recent years there have been such rapid and basic changes in our culture that our family life is vastly different. Today's parents need to be aware of those changes and to be sure that the life skills they teach, and the way they teach them, are in touch with the realities of today's culture, particularly as they affect today's family life. Three changes leap out at us.

1. Our culture has become far more complex.

The **traditional roles** of men, women, and children, formerly quite separate, fixed, simple, and predictable, have become quite overlapping, fluid, complex, unpredictable. The man used to earn the family money by having a full-time job, usually away from home. The woman was a housewife and mother who stayed home full-time, raised the children, did all the housework, and pretty much managed the home except perhaps for making major money decisions. The children went to school, did a few odd jobs around the house, and once their formal education was completed, left home for full-time work and then marriage.

Those roles have shifted dramatically and in complex ways. Even in the so-called traditional nuclear family of husband, wife, and children, the man often shares far more now in parenting and in housework. The woman often has a part-time or full-time job outside the home, including perhaps a prestigious position in business, government, or in the professions; she might well earn more money than her husband does. The children are involved in numerous activities outside the home: in school-sponsored athletics, debate, music; in nonschool activities such as private music lessons or ballet; in part-time jobs that often verge on full-time (in fast-food restaurants, or in hospitals, for instance, or in rock groups whose rehearsals and engagements eat up a huge amount of time outside the home).

In recent years. many people have embraced **situation ethics,** which emphasizes making moral decisions only after considering all the concrete circumstances of each concrete situation rather than relying on supposedly clear and universally accepted principles of right and wrong. Hence decision making in moral matters now seems immeasurably more complex than it was when a few simple rules or unquestioned proverbs such as "Spare the rod and spoil the child" or "The woman's place is in the home" seemed to give almost automatic answers.

This shifting of traditional roles and the popularity of situation ethics have together presented adults and children alike with far more numerous and complex choices than ever before. (**Should** the mother take this job outside the home? **Should** kids be "seen and not heard?") The huge array of choices has in turn created so-called **option stress** that seldom bothered our ancestors. Option stress comes about when we must make choices but lack adequate information to make those choices. Parents who honestly want to face today's complex world and to teach their kids life skills for dealing with it must be prepared to handle that new and often bewildering complexity and the stress that goes with it.

2. Kids are growing up sooner.

Experts tell us that kids are entering adolescence at age 9 or 10; that puberty, both physically and psychologically, begins as much as three years earlier than it did when most of us were growing up. Today, ten-year-olds are making critical, adult-level decisions such as whether to use alcohol or other drugs. Clearly, then, we must teach them important life skills much earlier.

3. Parents have less time to spend with their children.

Over two-thirds of our kids now live in homes where not even one parent is there full-time. In many two-parent families, economic necessity demands that both parents work; in single-parent families, which are increasingly common, the parent is far more likely to have a full-time job outside the home. What all this means is that parents must plan more carefully than ever to make the most of the precious time that is available to spend with their kids.

Many of us may feel inadequate as parents or feel guilty about maintaining the job schedules required to support a family. We may question our values and judgment. We may even consider changing our lifestyle to allow more time with our kids. Many, in fact, are choosing to do this, earning less but being home more.

Still, we need to know that just "being there more" won't necessarily make a difference. What's important is that we spend a reasonable amount of our available time building our relationships with our kids and teaching them the life skills they must have to grow up as mature, self-fulfilled adults. I hope the following pages on teaching life skills will help parents use their limited time efficiently and productively.

Methods of Teaching Life Skills: Basic Terms

Since Part 2 deals with various methods of teaching life skills to our kids, certain terms referring to those methods will constantly recur. So I want to clarify right now what I mean by those terms and why I think they're important. Here are the basic ones.

Modeling

Modeling refers to **exemplifying** in our own life the life skills we want to teach, as distinguished from merely explaining those skills and/or urging our kids to develop and use them. For instance, if we make our own decisions impulsively and only for short-term gains—for example, spending $300 we can't afford on a dress we'll probably wear only once or twice—we're in effect telling our kids, "That's the way to make decisions." Since our kids tend to mimic us, modeling is the most powerful of all teaching tools, for good or ill, as popular sayings correctly remind us: "Practice what you preach"; "Actions speak louder than words"; or, as it's sometimes rather ominously worded, "What you are speaks so loudly I can't hear what you're saying."

Reinforcement

Reinforcement refers to the practice of "catching them doing it right." When our kids demonstrate that they can effectively perform a certain life skill, we reinforce or strengthen them in that desirable behavior by praising them immediately and openly. ("I'm really impressed by the way you've been hitting those books at night. It shows you're looking ahead and seeing what that's going to mean in the long run.") The praise can be given also by nonverbal gestures such as a hug, a literal pat on the back, a handshake, a thumbs-up gesture. Reinforcement is one of the most important teaching tools available to parents.

Consistency

This term refers to our steadiness in the messages we send to our kids. We need to be unwavering and therefore predictable in those messages, since none of us can learn a game if the rules are always changing. If we tell our kids on Tuesday that feelings are their friends, we mustn't ridicule them on Thursday for feeling and expressing sadness or fear. ("Oh, don't be such a baby. It's only a football game.")

When we're consistent in what we teach our kids, they develop a sense of security that encourages them to try out new life skills that otherwise might intimidate them. For instance, when we consistently practice effective communication skills, we eventually find that kids not only open up more to us, but that they also begin to demonstrate effective communication skills with others.

Encouraging Practice of Life Skills

Practicing a new life skill in a low-risk setting within the family is an important preparation for transferring the learning to situations our kids will find at school with friends and in society generally. For instance, if we help our kids with the steps of decision making about saving money or choosing extracurricular activities, those same decision-making skills will be easier to use in riskier situations such as whether to drink alcohol with friends.

Techniques such as role playing or working with puppets to act out conversations or to discuss the pros and cons of life situations seen on TV will give kids a chance to think and to use various skills they'll need in real-life situations. For instance, recently, when my son and I were watching one of his favorite videos, "Swiss Family Robinson," we talked about the feelings of the family at Christmas when they thought the two older boys had been captured by pirates. The experience provided him with a safe environment in which to practice identifying and sharing some feelings that are often hard to deal with: anxiety and fear.

In short, allowing our kids opportunities to play with situations that represent real life for them gives them a safe but effective laboratory for practicing new life skills.

Allowing Mistakes

Whatever skill we try to learn, whether it's riding a bike or making decisions, we're going to mess up once in awhile. If kids are to learn new skills, they've got to know it's okay to make mistakes. We must develop a hands-off policy (no matter how itchy our hands get) that lets them skin a knee or once in awhile suffer the consequences of poor decision making until they learn to make sound decisions. Allowing some mistakes, however, doesn't mean totally disregarding their activities. A parent must always be there as a guide, a resource, a shoulder to lean on.

Patience

Working with kids, especially our own, requires tons of patience. Recently as I watched our two kids asleep and looking like a pair of angels, I could hardly imagine myself ever losing patience with them. But just four hours earlier those same two kids had driven me to the point where I was about ready to throw overboard all I'd ever learned about parenting. They were racing wildly down a supermarket aisle, playing pirate and waving make-believe swords. I could picture one of them knocking over a display of ketchup and see myself explaining to the manager how it had happened.

Patience seems like a gift that some of us have and others don't. Wrong. Patience is like a muscle. Some of us are given more muscle than others, but with exercise we can all develop it. In parenting my kids, the "Serenity Prayer" has helped me immensely in developing my "patience muscle." I find that instead of counting to ten, I rely on that simple prayer to help me muster at least enough patience to finish this shopping trip, get the kids and myself home, and live one more day with the satisfaction that I'm doing a pretty good job of being a parent.

Here's the prayer:

"God, grant me the serenity to accept the things
I cannot change, the courage to change the things
I can, and the wisdom to know the difference."

6

Feeling-Processing Skills

Rick has just broken up with Sarah, his girlfriend. Overwhelming feelings of sadness, hurt, and anger all form one huge ball in his stomach. He can't talk to anyone. He's too embarrassed to share his feelings, and he wouldn't know what to say if he did try to express them.

In school he sees Jerry, who's well known for using alcohol and other drugs. Rick starts a conversation with him and even eventually says he'd like to get high. Jerry sells him two marijuana joints and offers to smoke them with him.

Why did Rick so easily turn to marijuana? An obvious, easy explanation is that he was feeling bad and was looking for something that would help him feel better—and right now. Alcohol and other drugs do fill that bill: they do make us feel better right now. A deeper, more helpful explanation is that Rick lacked the cluster of life skills (called feeling-processing skills) that would have enabled him to deal with his feelings, especially with his uncomfortable, painful feelings. But that's by no means the whole answer either, for behind Rick's difficulty in handling feelings is a long, tangled tradition that Rick inherited: the human race's inability to understand and handle feelings.

Our Mysterious Feelings

To start with, let it be clear that our feelings are **bodily responses** that originated in our ancestors' instinctive physical responses to the world about them—for instance, in the fight-or-flight instinct we all still experience when we sense danger stalking us. We've all noticed the physical responses characteristic of deep feelings, such as quick breaths, pounding heart, clenched fists. Our everyday language, too, recognizes the physical basis of feelings: When we mention our "gut reaction" to something, we're speaking quite precisely. Feelings are very much of the body. And there's the rub. These bodily, animal reactions of ours are very familiar and yet very mysterious and disturbing. Like the wild animals themselves, they're immensely powerful, unpredictable, hard to control. Over the centuries, then, we humans have often handled them in inappropriate ways. Sometimes we've given in totally to their urgings and indulged in orgies of drunkenness, sex, or wholesale slaughter. At other times, frightened by those excesses, we've tried to suppress our feelings entirely, pretend they don't even exist, or at best have been quite suspicious of them.

In recent decades our culture has been struggling to give feelings their proper role in a balanced life, but the old battle goes on; and frankly, most of today's kids know very little about feelings and how to handle them. That's precisely why we need to help them develop life skills in that crucial area: When kids are tempted to get into alcohol or other drugs, they're almost invariably having problems with their feelings, not with their intellects.

The Three Stages of Processing Our Feelings

To get down to basics in understanding feelings and helping our kids understand them and deal successfully with them, let's talk about the three stages we need to go through to reach some mastery in this area: identifying feelings, owning them, and expressing (sharing) them.

Identifying Feelings

As we've mentioned, it's often quite easy to know when others are experiencing feelings, especially deep ones. Flashing eyes, scowls, a red face can be sure tip-offs. But when we're all stirred up inside, what are we really feeling? Recognizing and identifying our own feelings can be very difficult. Younger kids usually have to settle for something vague such as "I feel ishy" or "I feel bad." With help, though, even preschoolers can master simple ways of naming their feelings: "mad," "sad," "glad," for instance.

Once kids move into grade school they can usually begin to recognize and identify a wider range of feelings. Here's a sample.

Feeling Words

afraid	elated	irritated	satisfied
aggressive	enraged	jealous	scared
alarmed	enthusiastic	joyful	secure
amused	envious	lonely	shocked
angry	exasperated	loved	smug
annoyed	excited	mad	surprised
anxious	frightened	miserable	tense
appreciated	frustrated	needed	terrified
bitter	furious	nervous	threatened
bored	glad	paranoid	thrilled
calm	guilty	perplexed	troubled
cautious	happy	powerful	uneasy
comfortable	helpless	powerless	unimportant
concerned	hopeful	puzzled	unloved
confident	hopeless	regretful	unneeded
confused	horrified	rejected	unsure
contented	hostile	relieved	wanted
crushed	hurt	resentful	worried
disappointed	inadequate	respected	worthless
discouraged	inspired	sad	worthwhile
eager	insecure	safe	

As kids develop their capacity to recognize and identify feelings, it's important that we expose them to an increasingly larger vocabulary of feeling words. A simple exercise for kids is to take a list of such words and draw a face next to each. For instance:

happy

sad

It's amazing how even very young kids (grades 1-3) will be able to draw faces to match specific feelings.

Such an exercise not only helps kids to learn what a broad range of feelings we actually experience; it also helps them to identify their feelings and to move to the next stage of processing their feelings: owning them.

Owning Feelings

By "owning" feelings we simply mean acknowledging them as **ours,** acknowledging that they spring from **us** and are a part of **us.** Whether someone insults us and we react by feeling angry or embarrassed, or whether someone praises us and we react by feeling elated, what results is **our** feeling.

That may sound obvious, but it isn't. What often happens is that we in effect act as if our feeling is ultimately the responsibility of the **other** person. Laura says to Jack, "You made me mad because you said I cheated on the math exam, and I didn't." While we can sympathize with such an outburst, we need to recognize that blaming our feeling on someone else, making it the other's "property," is a cop-out. Why? Well, suppose Jack made the very same accusation against Jeanne, but Jeanne very calmly (though firmly) denied it, with no anger.

Since she came up with a response different from Laura's, it couldn't be merely Jack's accusation that **made** Laura angry; what made the difference was **Laura's** reaction: the way **she** took it and responded to it.

What that means is that we, not others, are ultimately responsible for our feelings. It's a hard lesson to learn, but it's true, and as we help our kids to see and accept that truth, we're showing them how to take control of their own lives: I'm the one who decides how I feel and act; I'm not at the mercy of what others decide about how I'm going to feel and act. At the same time, of course, the comforting realization that I'm in control of my own life means that I'm accepting **responsibility** for my feelings. That's a big step toward maturity.

We can also help our kids see that their feelings are their friends. How? By showing them that their feelings send them signals about how they're relating at the moment to persons, places, things, or circumstances. Teach them to ask themselves questions such as, **How** do I feel these days about my appearance? If I feel lousy about it, why? Am I just imagining that I'm too fat or that my clothes aren't right? And what's **behind** my feelings? Maybe I do need to eat healthier, non-fattening foods; maybe I do need some sound advice on how to dress; maybe I do need to wear less makeup or to buy clothes that work for me, not for someone else. How do I feel about my classes? If I'm feeling pretty happy, maybe my feelings are signaling me that I'm a conscientious kid who deserves to feel good about my studies.

When we discuss other life skills, such as those dealing with mood maintenance and decision making, we'll see more and more clearly how owning our feelings is indeed one of the primary life skills. Our next step, though, is to learn how to express (to share) our feelings.

Expressing Feelings

We can, of course, express our feelings in many ways: in artworks, poetry, stories, music. But it's absolutely imperative that our kids develop skills in expressing their feelings in the way in which practically everyone expresses them every day: by the spoken word. Learning to say out loud "I feel hurt" or "I feel good" is a fundamental life skill, because without the ability to verbalize our feelings we'll find ourselves alone, cut off from the support and concern that only relationships with people can provide. And those relationships depend heavily on our ability to communicate our feelings in spoken words.

By learning to express feelings, we're reaching out to others and building a bridge that creates the intimacy, togetherness, rapport, and mutual support we all need. Kids who can't **express** their feelings by talking about them are clearly more vulnerable to using alcohol and other drugs in order to **change** their feelings.

The following section on how to help kids process their feelings contains suggestions that apply to all three stages: identifying feelings, owning them, and expressing (sharing) them.

How to Help Kids Process Feelings

Things to Do

- An easy tool to help kids and to help ourselves to model appropriate handling of feelings is "I statements" such as "I feel hurt," "I feel happy," "I feel afraid." These "I statements" are nothing more than statements that begin with "I," name a feeling, and give a brief explanation. For instance, "I felt let down when I found you hadn't finished raking the lawn before you went out with Rick." By modeling statements that show we can identify, own, and express our feelings, we're teaching our kids a basic life skill.

- Help kids to identify their feelings by mentioning feelings they seem to be having. "You look sad today." Want to talk about it?" "You're smiling a lot today. You're happy about something."

- Read stories focusing on certain feelings; then talk about those feelings. *The Velveteen Rabbit, Charlotte's Web,* and *Winnie the Pooh* come to mind. Such stories contain many examples of how the characters live through situations that trigger important feelings. For instance, in *Charlotte's Web,* when Charlotte is concerned about Wilbur, her barnyard friend, we can talk about feelings associated with loyalty, fear, and perseverance. Stories are especially useful because all of us, and especially kids, usually have a much easier time identifying someone else's feelings.

- Have kids describe the feelings they get from a certain situation. For instance, have kids cut out pictures from old magazines and do a collage depicting how they felt when the home team won the basketball championship or how they felt the day they moved into the new house or when they didn't make the team. Younger kids (age 6-11) usually love to cut and paste, and even older kids (junior high and high schoolers) enjoy this activity. Pictures found in magazines and pasted on a sheet will often allow the more nonverbal kids to develop the skills they need to express their feelings openly.

- Expose kids to a rich, constructive vocabulary of feeling words. One way is to give them a sheet of feeling words and discuss them together.

- Be a good listener. Often our kids primarily need a sounding board for their feelings.

- Set aside some time each day for shutting off TVs, computer games, and music that interfere with free expression of feelings at home.

- Support kids when they express feelings. Frank statements such as "I'm glad you could tell me that," or nonverbal support such as hugs make a real impact on our kids.

- Be patient with kids' direct or indirect expressions of feelings ("I hate you" versus slamming the door or using sarcasm). Help them identify the feeling; invite them to share. ("You seem really angry. Can you talk to me about it?") Sometimes they find it difficult or impossible to share certain feelings with parents, so give them a chance to talk with others. They need a wide range of options. For instance, when Jean broke up with her boyfriend she chose to share the feelings with Aunt Susan. Though this was difficult for her mother to accept, it was easier for Jean to talk with her aunt than with her mother at that point in her life. What was important was that she was talking.

Things to Avoid

- Don't make judgments about feelings. Feelings are never good or bad. ("It's silly to feel that way.")

- Don't set consequences when kids are sharing their feelings honestly. Avoid any language or action that might seem like a threat or punishment. ("You might feel sorry now, but you'll be a lot sorrier when I'm finished with you.")

- Don't dominate the conversation. It's one thing to be a good model; it's another to take over. Appropriate sharing is fine, but when kids have feelings it's important to let them own them. ("I know exactly how you feel. Last week at work when Jerry . . ."— and the parent rambles on and on with his or her own story, forgetting the youngster's problem.)

- Avoid rescuing. Kids have to own their feelings and eventually make their decision about how to deal with them. Being sensitive and supportive doesn't mean rescuing. ("You'll feel better if I take you to a movie.")

Summary

Processing feelings is a cluster of life skills that we must help our kids learn if we want to prevent them from saying yes to alcohol and other drugs, because critical decisions about alcohol and other drugs are made, as we've pointed out, in emotionally charged situations. The typical youngster really hasn't been given much understanding of feelings: what they are, how they influence us, what we can do not only to counter their possible harm to us but to use them in a positive way as our friends and powerful helpers in developing a well-balanced, strong personality.

Kids whose parents have explained feelings to them and helped them put their knowledge to work in everyday home situations will be able to identify their feelings, own them, and express them in a healthy, constructive way. Such kids are in a strong position to make important decisions wisely and firmly.

Finally, because feelings pervade our whole life, handling them well is basic to developing the other life skills that we now go on to discuss.

7

Decision-Making Skills

Shawn, a seventh grader, is walking to school with his friend Brian. Brian suggests that they skip school and go to the video arcade, then go to Brian's house and drink a few beers. He's pretty sure his parents won't miss the beers because there's a whole case of cans opened in the basement, and his parents aren't the kind to keep close track of them. Brian says, "It'll be a blast, and no one will ever know the difference. I can get my older sister to write us excuses for school and sign our parents' names to them."

Brian has been his friend since grade school, and Shawn knows it would be fun. But he also realizes that if they get caught he could be in a lot of trouble. Shawn has to make a decision.

The ability to make wise decisions is more critical than ever for today's kids, who are faced with making very adult decisions at an increasingly younger age. For instance, as we noted earlier, one-third of our kids report feeling "some" to "a lot" of peer pressure to use alcohol and other drugs by the time they're in fourth grade. This means that by that time they already need to be comfortable using decision-making skills when they're confronted with such adult level choices as whether to use alcohol or other drugs.

Components of Decision Making

To help our kids develop skill in decision making, we need to be clear in our own minds—and to make clear to them—the four basic components of the process: identifying our feelings, brainstorming, sorting out pros and cons, and evaluating those pros and cons.

Identifying Feelings

As I mentioned in Chapter 6, processing feelings is a basic skill upon which other life skills such as decision making are based. The first stage of processing, that of identifying feelings, is particularly relevant to decision making. When Shawn is confronted by Brian's invitation, what he needs to do first is identify his own feelings. If he's able to do that he might identify several conflicting ones.

- I like Brian and want to keep him as a friend, and I'm afraid I might lose him if I don't skip school with him.

- It'd be fun to skip school.

- I'm afraid of what might happen if we got caught.

- I'd feel guilty and scared about skipping school, drinking stolen beer, handing in a fake excuse at school, and lying to my parents.

Primarily, Brian feels afraid that he might lose a friend. When he considers skipping school and drinking beer to keep his friend, he anticipates that he might feel excited, afraid, and guilty.

Decisions typically have their roots in many such complex and ambivalent feelings. Some decisions are based on feelings we have right now, others on feelings we've had in the past, still others on feelings we predict we'll have in the future. Since our feelings are so complex and even contradictory, we need to sort them out carefully and name them clearly so that we know just what they are.

After we've identified them we're ready to move on to the next step in decision making—brainstorming.

Brainstorming

Brainstorming is nothing more than thinking and perhaps listing in writing the options available in a given situation.

Shawn, for instance, clearly has two primary options: either skip school or go to school. As he continues to consider options, though, others might become clear.

- He could refuse to join Brian altogether and go on to school.

- He could go to school in the morning and meet Brian at noon.

- He could skip school but not drink the beer with Brian.

- He could try to persuade Brian not to drink the beer.

- He could try to persuade Brian not to skip school.

Sorting Out Pros and Cons

The options are really quite numerous. Each option has consequences, both positive and negative, that would probably follow. We often refer to these anticipated consequences as pros and cons of the choice. As we discussed in Chapter 5, it's important that we raise kids in an environment in which considering the mixed consequences of our choices is a normal, natural part of everyday life. I've discovered again and again in dealing with kids that teaching them to sort out the pros and cons of their decisions is very helpful. As Shawn, for instance, ponders his options he can rather easily sort them out on that basis.

His pros for skipping school with Brian might well be:

- It would be fun.

- Brian might accept me more.

- I could brag about it to other kids.

His cons might well be:

- I might get in trouble at school.

- I might lose privileges at home.

- I'd feel guilty lying at home and at school.

- I'd feel guilty about drinking beer when I know my parents object.

- I'd feel guilty about drinking stolen beer.

- Some kids at school might think I was stupid.

It might seem clear to you and me that the cons far outweigh the pros, but how Shawn decides will depend on the next step: how he evaluates their relative weights.

Evaluating Pros and Cons

This step is the climax of the decision-making process. After all, no matter how right or wrong our decision might prove to be, we ultimately make it on the basis of how we evaluate the pros and cons. In effect we say, "All things considered, this set looks more attractive than that set. So I'm going **this** way." Here are several things we can do to help our kids evaluate pros and cons wisely.

1. When we look at Shawn's lists of pros and cons, we notice right away that most of the pros for skipping school bring immediate rewards such as having fun and being accepted by his peers. But all the cons bring delayed consequences such as feelings of guilt and fear of being caught. If Shawn makes his choice on the basis of what will feel best right now (immediate gratification), he might choose to skip school. But as he learns to forgo immediate gratification for longer-term benefits, he'll very probably opt to go to school. While it's difficult for young people to think beyond this moment, it's possible with practice and guidance from parents. The message to us is clear: to help kids make choices to say no to alcohol and other drugs, we must help them learn to consider long-range consequences.

2. To help kids learn how to evaluate pros and cons, we also need to teach them to consider those pros and cons from a variety of perspectives. For instance:

- The perspective of one's best self alone: In view of my own values, regardless of what others think or of whatever else might happen, which decision will I be proudest of?

- The perspective of others: In view of what my parents, friends, and others might think and do (in other words, my reputation and the consequences that others might inflict on me), which decision will I be most comfortable with?

- The long-range perspective: When I think not just of today but of tomorrow, next week, next month, even years from now, which decision will I feel best about?

3. It's difficult for kids to think about the future and to develop the habit of anticipating that every decision they make will have either immediate or eventual consequences or both. So we need to be very patient in helping them develop this crucial life skill. But my experience has been that with patience and practice, kids can slowly develop the ability to make choices that have positive long-term results.

4. We need more than patience. We need to keep thinking of practical ways of helping our kids learn this skill. That means weaving decision making into the fabric of our everyday family life so that it becomes an integral, expected part of their life. After all, if the only decisions our kids make are huge, career-threatening or life-threatening ones such as the decision to use or not use alcohol and other drugs (decisions typically made away from home, where our influence is far weaker), they won't have developed the necessary skills to handle such major tasks all at once, and we can almost predict they'll choose poorly.

Here are some practical ways of helping them develop this skill.

How to Help Kids Make Decisions

Things to Do

- Model good decision making. Talk to kids about decisions you're faced with, and explain the steps you go through in making a decision. (For instance: joining or not joining the PTA, buying a car or house, choosing a vacation time and place, changing jobs.) Ask them to help you identify your feelings, brainstorm your options, sort out and then evaluate pros and cons. Allow them to become involved in the decisions we adults face.

- Be a resource. Rather than giving kids solutions or directions because we're sure we know what's best, be there as a resource to help them go through the four big steps in making their own decisions. (For instance: choices of friends, whom to date, extracurricular activities, part-time jobs, spending their money.) Mark is faced with whether to save his earnings for a car or to take a trip out West with friends. Let him make the choice, but help him sort out his options and their long-term ramifications.

- Encourage kids to investigate pros and cons by playing "what if." They enjoy the game, and it's an education. (For instance: What if I ask the girl my

best friend likes to go to the game with me? What
if I'm asked to be a cheerleader and my best friend
isn't? What if the boy I like wants me to smoke a
joint? What if my best friend shoplifts while I'm
with her?)

- Allow kids to make mistakes. We'd never learn to
  ride a bike if we didn't risk a few spills. So allow
  kids to make some choices you don't really agree
  with. (For instance, Joey decides to quit his after-
  school job as a result of an argument with his boss.
  You may think it's a mistake, but Joey has to make
  the choice. Of course, if he has agreed to have an
  after-school job in order to earn his own spending
  money, he'll be expected to look for another one.)

- Encourage kids to get involved in a personal-
  growth group, or in various activities in which
  they'll have opportunities to make decisions and
  help others make decisions. (For instance: church
  youth groups, Scouting programs, personal-growth
  groups, youth leadership groups such as student
  council, Kiwanis Key Club, and other youth
  service organizations.)

- Look for opportunities to discuss decision making
  with your kids, especially in a risk-free
  environment where unwise choices don't really do
  any harm. TV programs, movies, books, comic
  books, the daily newspaper all offer many
  opportunities to second-guess choices others have

made. (For instance, a few from books: Was Peter Rabbit smart in leaving the briar patch that day? Was Little Red Riding Hood smart going into the forest alone? Should Huck Finn have left home?) It's easy to choose examples to fit the age and capacities of the kids, on topics ranging from little decisions made in kids' stories to major decisions about marriage, divorce, world poverty and hunger, war, and global environmental problems, not to mention decisions that famous athletes and entertainers have made about using alcohol and other drugs.

- Be interested in longer-term outcomes of what kids are doing. Give them encouragement by praise and other rewards for completing projects or activities they've begun; many kids have great initial enthusiasm but soon give up. (For instance: Encourage kids who persevere in building a model airplane, in sticking with piano lessons or art projects, or saving money for a long-term purchase.)

- Actually work side by side with your kids in projects that require a long time, stamina, and patience to complete. (For instance: building a model car, becoming involved in a hobby such as fishing, woodworking, sewing, or needlecraft.) As the project unfolds, help them be invested in it by asking them how they think the two of you should go about it, and by letting them make critical choices on such matters as selecting materials and colors. Encourage them by praising their enthusiasm, their self-discipline, their perseverance in sticking with a difficult, lengthy task.

Things to Avoid

- Don't make decisions your kids should make, such as whom to date, what clothes to buy, whether to save money for school or buy the new CD player. Even though we probably know what's best for them, it's never productive to interfere in choices that are truly their responsibility. (See Chapters 5 and 6 on which responsibilities belong to parents, which to kids.) The goal of parenting, after all, is to prepare kids to face the real world. So we have to involve them in situations where they learn real life skills that will actually help them deal effectively with everyday situations. By learning the importance of being on time for school, football practice, or baby-sitting jobs, they're developing the skills to succeed in their first full-time job, where the stakes suddenly have become much higher.

- Don't lecture. Listen. Our role in the process of our kids' decision making is essentially that of being a resource and a sounding board. Don't become the authority. Kids learn only by doing. Only if John decides to save money for a long-term purchase will it really mean anything to him. Otherwise it's just another example of doing "what the Old Man makes me do."

Summary

For kids to avoid alcohol and other drugs they must be prepared to make even major decisions at a very early age. As I've mentioned, we must assume that by age 8 or 9 our kids may have to make critical choices related to alcohol and other drug use. These choices are complex and emotionally charged. Simplistic short-term solutions will always fall short. Kids must be equipped to make choices that will benefit them in the long run.

As we look at the next life skill, establishing positive behavior, it will become obvious how feeling-processing skills and decision-making skills combine to provide a positive framework for kids to manage their own behavior.

8

Skills for Establishing Positive Behavior

Some kids seem almost immune to problems. No matter what happens, they take it in stride. While other kids seem trapped in difficulty after difficulty, these kids seem to have been gifted with some special quality that shields them.

Consider, by contrast, Mary, age 15. She tries out for cheerleader but doesn't make it. Overwhelmed with feelings of anger, hurt, and frustration, but lacking the life skills that would enable her to deal with her feelings, she withdraws into herself, silently angry. But she pretends that everything is all right. When Ron, a heavy alcohol and other drug user, asks her to go to a kegger that night, she immediately accepts, thinking only of her need to find something to make her feel better **now.**

Once she loses her inhibitions by drinking, her behavior at the kegger is loud and aggressive. She accuses the girls who made the cheerleader squad of being two-faced and phony. She drinks too much and passes out. Ron deposits her at her doorstep very late that night.

Her parents are livid; Mary is sick. Her self-image is in the pits, and she feels worse than before. She retreats farther into herself and feels alone and afraid.

How could this have happened? Mary has been caught in a pattern of behavior that feeds on itself. Her inability to deal effectively with her feelings, coupled with a faulty decision-making process that considered only immediate needs, has led her to behavior that in the short haul is self-defeating and in the long haul is potentially self-destructive. This behavior in turn has produced stronger negative feelings such as guilt, self-doubt, and low self-esteem. It also has created an increasing desire to escape by means of any behavior that produces immediate results. More specifically, her initial feelings (anger, hurt, and frustration) led to a decision to get immediate relief from those feelings, which in turn led to behavior involving drug use, which led Mary back to feelings that were even more negative: guilt, self-doubt, and low self-esteem. These negative feelings will feed into a circular pattern that results in self-destructive behavior.

The pattern closely resembles the one shown in the following diagram.

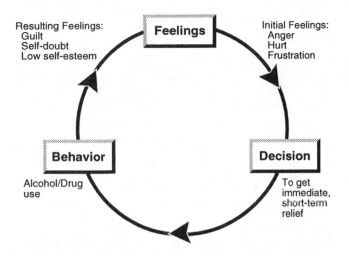

As I've repeatedly emphasized in this book, the key to avoiding such a pattern lies in developing a whole array of positive life skills that will prevent the pattern from ever getting started. (Sad experience has shown that adolescents who lack those life skills run a significantly higher risk of developing alcohol or other drug dependence.) We've already discussed two of them, processing feelings and making decisions, and we're ready for the third: establishing positive patterns of behavior.

Most negative behavior patterns that youngsters develop begin in situations that deeply affect their feelings. Such experiences as breaking up with a boyfriend or girlfriend, getting a bad grade, not making the team, or being shunned by a friend can be emotionally devastating for a kid. The challenge for us is to show our kids how to establish positive patterns of behavior. The first two elements in such patterns are the two we've already discussed in Chapters 6 and 7 respectively, and even at the risk of seeming to be repetitious, I must very briefly refer to them here to show how they fit into the positive patterns.

Processing Feelings and Making Decisions

Let's assume that a youngster has learned those two bedrock life skills of processing feelings and making wise decisions. As those two skills develop, kids gradually begin making choices that will prove sensible in the long run (they're overcoming the tendency to choose only on the basis of immediate gratification). For instance, when Mike learned he had been cut from the football team, he was naturally crushed. But he talked his feelings out with parents and friends and decided to join an early fall basketball team instead. Now he's working his way toward a successful basketball season rather than becoming caught up in self-defeating behavior as a result of being cut from the football team. In other words, Mike has learned to turn problems into opportunities. This means he's already well on his way to establishing positive patterns of behavior. Here are three other major ways of ensuring that he'll follow through on his decisions in such a way as to enlarge and deepen this positive pattern:

- establishing and maintaining a positive attitude

- developing and sticking to an action plan

- learning to congratulate oneself.

Establishing and Maintaining Positive Attitudes

Kids who get caught in self-defeating patterns of **behavior** often also get caught up in self-defeating **attitudes** toward themselves.

An attitude is one's general disposition toward a person, place, or thing. For example, second-grade boys often have an attitude toward girls that is quite critical, judgmental, harsh. "Girls are dumb" pretty well sums it up. This attitude will generally take a 180° turn by the time they've reached seventh grade.

Our most important attitudes are those we have toward ourselves. Overly harsh, critical, judgmental attitudes about ourselves are self-defeating.

A good way of becoming aware of our attitudes about ourselves is to look at **how we talk to ourselves.** Kids who get caught in self-defeating attitudes most often say things to themselves like:

- "I'm just too dumb."
- "I'm too ugly."
- "I'm too slow."
- "No one cares about me."
- "Nothing matters anyway."

These patterns of negative self-talk reinforce patterns of self-defeating behavior because they provide an immediate excuse or rationalization for it. And naturally they also keep the young person trapped.

151

The key to learning self-enhancing behavior lies in **establishing an attitude that reflects confidence, openness, and a willingness to try.** A helpful way to build up that positive attitude is to help kids learn to use **affirmations.** Affirmations are short, usually one-line statements that reflect encouraging, self-enhancing self-talk. For instance:

- "I'm a good person."

- "I'm a lovable person."

- "I'm a hard worker."

- "I do good things."

- "I can do almost anything I set my mind to."

- "I like people."

- "I'm growing."

We can also derive positive affirmations from stories, spiritual readings, songs, and many other sources. For instance, the song "Raindrops Keep Fallin' on My Head," the children's book *The Little Engine That Could,* the adults' book *Jonathan Livingston Seagull,* and the "Serenity Prayer," cited in the Introduction to Part 2, are full of such affirmations.

How we talk to ourselves is clearly related to **the attitude we project to others.** If we can learn to talk to ourselves in a confident, patient, and supportive tone, we'll begin to project our attitude to others. For instance, first graders who have learned to chant "Sticks and stones will break my bones but words will never hurt me" have learned how a simple affirmation can help make them immune to name-calling. This simple affirmation has given strength and confidence to thousands of kids.

Learning to use affirmations helps us project an image of confidence and strength. This image in turn is the beginning of establishing positive, self-enhancing behavior patterns that help kids make difficult choices such as saying no to alcohol and other drugs.

The next step in helping our kids establish positive behavior patterns is to help them establish an action plan.

Establishing an Action Plan

An action plan is nothing more than the total of small doable steps into which we break a larger, more general goal or objective. These doable steps in turn provide the young person with small bits of success and positive payoffs along the way.

For instance, Mark decided to continue track even though he didn't make the relay team this year. After processing his feelings of disappointment and frustration, he made that decision mostly because he believed he had a strong chance of making the team next year. Now came the hard part: how to follow through with a plan that had few payoffs until perhaps a whole year later. The key was to establish a plan that broke the ultimate, larger goal into many action steps along the way. To do that, Mark made up a chart that allowed him to record his progress daily. As he participated in his regular workouts he was able to note his progress toward his overall goal and to experience positive feelings of pride, confidence, and excitement.

An additional element that Mark wove into his action plan was to take up a field event that no one else on the track team was entering (he chose shot put). This gave him the opportunity to participate in this year's scheduled meets and receive some immediate satisfaction from being in track **this** year.

Learning to establish an action plan is a skill that helps kids channel their activities in a direction that will create **long-term** rewards but also carry **short-term payoffs** along the way. By establishing self-enhancing patterns of behavior our kids are also building stronger self-esteem and generating positive feelings that in turn reinforce additional positive choices.

As this next diagram shows, patterns of **positive** behavior can become closely linked, mutually reinforcing, and habit forming, as our earlier diagram showed self-destructive behavior doing.

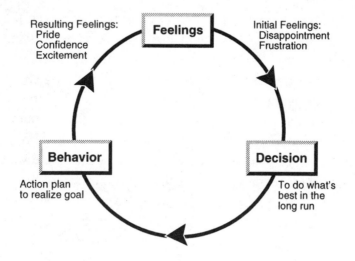

The final step of establishing positive patterns of behavior is that of learning to give ourselves a good pat on the back.

Congratulating Oneself

Our culture has a strong taboo against being a braggart. This taboo often prevents us from congratulating ourselves when we do well.

Learning to say to ourselves "Good job!" or "I did my best" or "I deserve this award (recognition, praise)" or "I did really well" is important to us if we hope to teach our kids these important ways of establishing positive patterns of behavior.

Note how cleverly beer companies pitch their TV commercials to capitalize on our reluctance to congratulate ourselves. They subtly congratulate us, letting us know we deserve a reward: "It's Miller time"; "It doesn't get any better than this"; This Bud's for you."

We need to be at least as congratulatory toward our kids as these commercials are to all of us. We need to show our kids how to build themselves up by patting themselves on the back: "John, you should pat yourself on the back for studying so hard." Kids can learn to congratulate themselves on many things. Learning how to handle money, choosing good companions, getting a part-time job after school, practicing the flute faithfully—the opportunities for realizing and acknowledging to themselves that they're developing as good persons are endless. And these are attainable, repeatable behaviors that they can perform; they don't all have to score the winning touchdown or get all A's and B's.

By teaching our kids to give themselves credit, we're not only building up their self-image; we're encouraging them to strive for solid achievement even when no one else seems to be aware of how well they're doing. A harsh reality of adult life is that many of our victories go unnoticed and unheralded. By helping our kids learn to reinforce **themselves** we help them be less dependent on constant reinforcement from others. Kids who are unhealthily dependent on the approval of others (especially of their peers) are the very ones who are vulnerable to peer pressure when the time comes to make decisions about using or not using alcohol and other drugs.

How to Help Kids Establish Positive Behavior

Things to Do

- Become more aware of our own patterns of behavior and try to model patterns that are healthy and self-enhancing. "I really feel good sticking with my exercise program this past month. The work is beginning to pay off." "Your dad and I have decided to have one evening a week for ourselves. We think it's important for us."

- Freely and openly say affirmations about kids. "I'm very impressed with how self-disciplined you are about doing outside reading." "I admire your willingness to practice the piano so regularly."

- Acknowledge kids' daily successes as they occur. Learning to pat ourselves on the back is first learned from others who pat us on the back. "You must be proud of that debate trophy."

- Teach kids to respond directly to positive feedback with simple acknowledgments such as "Thank you" and "I'm glad you like it" rather than denying or minimizing the congratulations with "It's really nothing; anyone could have done it."

- Work with kids to establish action plans they can share with you as they successfully carry through on activities. Such devices as using charts onto which you can post stars or other stickers work well with younger kids. Action plans can usually be developed into a chart listing specific behaviors ("Clean my room," "Get up on time,"). These specific behaviors can be marked off every day with a sticker.

- When confronting negative behavior be willing to go beyond just setting consequences. Help kids to understand which part of the process (feelings, decisions, or behavior) is causing them problems. For instance, when Kerstin started sleeping late after her fight with her boyfriend, her mom not only confronted the behavior but invited her out to breakfast the following Saturday to talk. During their discussion Kerstin began to see how her feelings about her boyfriend were affecting her behavior around the house. Kerstin developed a plan with her mom to change her behavior. She also realized that her mom really cared about her and was interested in more than just having her get up on time.

- Be openly demonstrative with praise that acknowledges some specific aspect of a kid. "It amazes me how much effort you've been putting into that history paper." Positive feelings, hugs, and congratulations from us often become much too rare, especially as our kids get older.

Things to Avoid

- Don't use money or material presents or exaggerated praise as rewards for positive behavior. These rewards undermine the establishment of the life skill for its own sake and give kids the unrealistic expectation that rewards always follow positive behavior.

- Don't give others credit for what your kids do. It can sometimes be easy to congratulate a coach, a team, a teacher, or anyone else for what our own kids accomplish. No matter who has helped, kids must receive credit directly from us for their good behavior, just as they receive blame for their negative behavior.

- Don't withhold approval. Sometimes we withhold it because we suspect our kids of being manipulative, or because they misbehaved yesterday, or because we're simply not comfortable giving praise. When our kids do something well they deserve to be congratulated. If we wait till they're perfect to praise them we'll be waiting a long time.

Summary

Establishing a pattern of positive behaviors is essential to preventing alcohol or other drug problems with our kids. Positive behavior can become self-perpetuating and self-enhancing just as truly and as powerfully as negative behavior such as alcohol and other drug use can. And when we teach our kids the whole array of life skills that I'm advocating in this book, we're giving them basic education in how to approach life's biggest problems with a confidence that brings success. Kids with such skills and such fundamental confidence are armed with the best preventive methods ever devised against alcohol and other drugs.

9

Mood-Maintenance Skills

Ben is stuck. He feels numb inside. When pushed to describe his feelings, he says he feels empty. He avoids decisions: He doesn't have the energy for thinking and analyzing. His behavior has become lethargic. He often sleeps 10 to 14 hours a day.

Ben is caught in a very low-range mood of depression. Unfortunately, kids who become engulfed in these low-range moods are extremely vulnerable to using alcohol and other drugs as a means of self-medication.

Lisa is also stuck, but on the other end of the spectrum. She's obsessively active, afraid to slow down or relax. Moving from activity to activity, Lisa uses perpetual motion as a way to avoid facing her feelings. Being a perfectionist, she's afraid that if she doesn't **always** make sure that things get done, and done very well, people will think bad things about her. Lately she's pushed herself beyond what she can handle. She's been experiencing frequent headaches and insomnia and has been lashing out at people with sarcastic, cutting responses. While she appears to be extremely popular and always on the go, she feels no satisfaction in what she does. In short, she finds herself trapped in the upper-range mood of anxiety.

What Are Moods?

Moods are sometimes described as the product of

- how we deal with our feelings
- decisions we make
- behaviors we participate in.

Individuals who become trapped in self-defeating patterns of dealing with feelings, decisions, and behaviors usually find themselves caught in either upper-range or low-range moods. That's a set-up for kids to use alcohol and other drugs, as we'll explain more fully.

In explaining moods to kids I often use the analogy of a car going from 0 to 100 miles per hour. The car speeds correspond to the following moods:

0	Depressed
10	Detached
20	Bored
30	Calm
40	Relaxed
50	Interested
60	Excited
70	Anxious
80	Irritable
90	Angry
100	Enraged

Most kids know that cars run most efficiently and safely at somewhere between 30 and 60 miles per hour, even though we sometimes need to drive them faster or slower.

The moods corresponding to speeds of from 30 to 60 miles per hour tend to be the safest and most productive for us humans as well. If we find ourselves stuck in the low-range moods of boredom, detachment, or depression, we never get anywhere. People around us become impatient, and eventually we lose all momentum and direction.

Conversely, if we get stuck in the high-range moods of anxiety, irritability, anger, or rage, we often go off half cocked, we can't slow down, and we usually run the risk of hurting ourselves or others.

Being stuck in these uncomfortable high or low mood ranges is easier than most of us think. If we lack the life skills to effectively process our feelings, make good decisions, or maintain productive behavior, we'll find ourselves more likely to become trapped in these uncomfortable moods. Moods are the product of how we deal with the challenges we face on a day-in, day-out basis. If we lack skills in any vital area of daily life, this void can severely affect our moods.

Kids and adults who get trapped in the low-range or high-range moods are usually victims of their inability to process feelings, make good decisions, and/or maintain productive patterns of behavior. Consequently, we might describe our moods as being encircled by the activities of feeling processing, decision making, and behavior control. By looking at moods in this way we begin to see that when we lack any one life skill, our moods will move to the high or the low range.

For instance, Jerry, age 9, has just come home again from playing with Larry and Ted. His mom can tell something has happened because he won't talk and just wants to stretch out in front of the TV. He looks upset and hurt, but he won't say a word. Jerry's mom knows this will be the beginning of a long evening of silence, because when Jerry sinks into these moods he refuses to talk and when pushed only lashes out with anger.

Jerry sank into this mood of detachment as a result of an argument with Larry and Ted. In the course of the argument Jerry's anger swelled to a point where he felt overwhelmed. He lashed out and hit Larry. Ted immediately intervened and restrained Jerry, so Jerry left in a huff.

Anger has always been a problem for Jerry. When things set him off he doesn't know what to do. Afterward he feels more anger, but he's also afraid. His natural tendency is to withdraw, to pull inward.

Jerry's moods swing uncontrollably from low range to high range because he lacks the skills to effectively process his feelings, make decisions, or manage his own behavior. This is a perfect setup for alcohol or other drug use.

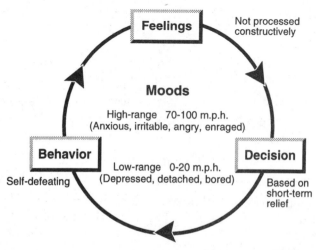

However, when kids learn life skills in the areas of feelings, decisions, and behavior, they process their feelings more effectively, make decisions based on long-term needs and goals, and follow through with self-enhancing behavior. When those things happen, their moods stabilize within that middle zone of 30 to 60 miles per hour—which means that they're calm, relaxed, interested, healthily excited. The following diagram sums up the situation.

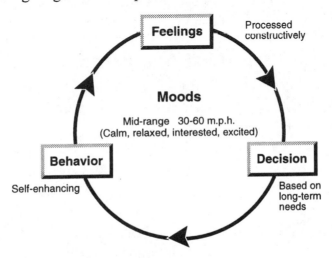

Moods and the Alcohol or Other Drug Problem

Kids who get caught in either the high-range or the low-range moods tend to run a greater risk of **early** abuse of alcohol or other drugs and also run a significantly high risk of developing serious problems with them.

As I explained in Chapter 2, alcohol and other drugs are attractive primarily because they can change our moods. Significantly, all the substances grouped under the heading of alcohol and other drugs are often referred to as mind or mood-altering chemicals. Kids (and adults) who find themselves without the life skills to maintain their moods in the middle range (30-60) often resort to mind-altering chemicals, seemingly in an attempt to self-medicate moods that have become uncomfortable.

In working with kids, we consistently find that those who have learned to maintain their moods within the middle range are less likely either to use alcohol and other drugs or to develop problems with them.

Strategies for Mood-Maintenance

The life skills discussed in Chapters 6, 7, and 8—processing feelings, making good decisions, and following through with appropriate behavior—are crucially important in helping kids to keep their moods in the middle range. Here are some other useful strategies by which parents can help their kids to reach that goal.

Diet

Getting sound nutrition on a daily basis is an essential ingredient in maintaining our moods. One foster mother I worked with explained that when Debbie ate nothing but junk food her moods also became junky. For her, poor eating habits were a sure-fire way of falling victim to the low-range moods of boredom and eventually depression. Almost all family physicians have literature on sound family nutrition. Or check out a book from the library or ask at your local bookstore.

Concerned parents need to be well informed on nutrition, incorporate their knowledge into the family's eating habits, and teach their kids the importance of a healthy diet.

Sleep

Many of the chemically dependent kids I've worked with have long histories of poor sleeping habits and sleep disturbances. Research has shown that school-age kids need at least 8-9 hours of sleep per night. Getting less than we need tends to have negative effects on our moods. When we're parents of infants we establish for them consistent habits associated with naps, bedtimes, going to sleep, and waking up. As our kids enter childhood and adolescence it's important that we continue to establish reasonable limits and have house rules that allow our kids the regular sleep they need. This also helps ensure that **others** will get their sleep.

A particularly troublesome trend of recent years has been that of younger kids 13-14 years old working in late-night restaurants until 1 or 2 A.M. Generally speaking, we shouldn't allow our children to work late shifts, especially on school nights. Some states, in fact, are considering legislation that would limit the hours that kids can work on school nights. These legislative efforts should be supported by anyone concerned about kids.

Exercise

Kids (and adults) suffering from problems with moods, especially low-range moods associated with depression, often are inactive. There's even a current term, "couch potatoes," that describes an emerging generation of inactives. "Couch potatoes" have made a career of watching life from the sidelines. Kids prone to being "couch potatoes" are often the victims of families that lack structure and planned activities, Instead, kids are left to fend for themselves—grazing on junk food and being "medicated" by endless hours of watching TV, playing video games, or listening to rock music.

Regular exercise not only keeps us fit; it also affects our moods and changes our whole outlook on life.

In clinical work with chronically depressed persons it's taken for granted that clinicians will set up a regular exercise program for them. Such a program is no less essential for the rest of us. When we exercise regularly ourselves and make it part of the whole family's schedule, we're heading off problems like serious depression. Regular exercise easily develops into a long-term habit that can help kids keep their moods in the middle range. Parents can develop a regular exercise program for themselves and invite the kids to participate regularly: walking, swimming, tennis, or volleyball, for instance. To exercise as a family at least three times a week is beneficial in two ways: it promotes quality family time, and it ensures proper exercise for all.

Relaxation

Relaxation is especially important for the child who has tendencies toward the high-range moods of anxiety, irritability, and rage. Activities that develop one's ability to relax—such as meditation, reading, and various crafts are important tools in mood-maintenance. Kids learn how to relax by seeing us relax doing activities that we enjoy, and by being allowed to participate in those activities with us. In our family we spend some evenings getting out the watercolors and painting. On other evenings it's play dough and clay. The important thing is the activity, not the quality of the product. Even something as simple as Saturday morning kite flying or going to the library together can give kids an invaluable lesson in the art of slowing down and doing something that's both fun and relaxing.

As we discover more about moods and how they're related to other aspects of our lives, it becomes increasingly clear how important it is to work with our kids to develop relaxation skills. For the young person who has natural tendencies toward the high-range moods, alcohol and other drugs pose a serious threat.

H.A.L.T.

Our six-year-old boy had just come home from the beach after an exciting afternoon there. As fatigue overtook his excitement, though, he gradually moved into the upper-range mood of irritability. He wanted a drink **right now,** and it had to be Sprite, not Pepsi (we were out of Sprite, naturally). Whines and sniffles. He didn't want to nap, even for a few minutes, and he wanted to watch "Sesame Street" **right now**—even though it wasn't on right now. And so it went. His poor mother was wondering "Did **we** do something wrong? And why isn't this child grateful for that nice outing at the beach?"

It's not only six year olds who have those mood swings. All of us do. Often without our even knowing it, our moods will move, for instance, from the high middle range (excitement) to the high range (irritability) or from the low middle range (calm) to the low range (boredom). Now, it's clear that unless we're aware of our moods and mood shifts, we're at the mercy of unknown forces that are pulling us in any direction they want. In such a situation we **can't** be in control of our own life.

A life skill that has been taught to thousands of recovering alcoholics as a means of making them aware of their mood swings is H.A.L.T. It's a technique we can easily teach ourselves and our kids. The letters stand for "hungry, angry, lonely, tired." Originally this system was used as a means for alcoholics to maintain their moods and consequently to avoid returning to alcohol or other drugs. The message for the alcoholic was and is to avoid getting too hungry, angry, lonely or tired, because that's a sure-fire way to fall back into alcohol or other drug use.

I've also used H.A.L.T. with kids as a tool to indicate that some strange, uncomfortable things may be going on inside them:

- **Hungry:** "I'm hungry even though I've eaten enough."

- **Angry:** "I'm angry even though there's no one bothering me."

- **Lonely:** "I'm lonely even though there are people all around me."

- **Tired:** "I'm tired even though I've had enough sleep."

When kids complain, for example, of feeling hungry even though they've clearly had enough to eat, H.A.L.T. is signaling that they're experiencing feelings they haven't identified, owned, and expressed constructively, and that as a result they're slipping from healthy mid-range moods to the more unstable high-range or low-range moods. Teaching our kids to be **aware** of their moods and mood changes is a long step toward helping them **maintain** those moods in the middle range, which puts them in a much stronger position to be able to say no to alcohol or other drugs.

Mood Diagram

Another strategy I use to help kids maintain their moods in the productive middle range is the mood diagram I mentioned briefly at the beginning of this chapter.

	Mood Diagram	
	Miles per hour	**Mood**
Low-range moods:	0	Depressed
	10	Detached
	20	Bored
	H.A.L.T.	
Mid-range moods:	30	Calm
	40	Relaxed
	50	Interested
	60	Excited
	H.A.L.T.	
High-range moods:	70	Anxious
	80	Irritable
	90	Angry
	100	Enraged

I use this diagram to help kids understand how both the kind and the intensity of their various activities affect their moods and to help them become aware of when they're moving from the mid-range to the high-range or low-range moods.

Furthermore, when kids become familiar with this diagram, they're better able to choose those activities that put them into or keep them in the comfortable middle range of moods and to avoid activities that put them in the uncomfortable low or high ranges. For instance, Brad, a client of mine, wanted to play football, but he wasn't really very good at it, so he spent most of his time on the bench. As a result, whether the team won or lost he came home depressed. When I discussed the mood diagram with him, he realized that his perceived failure in football was causing his depression. So he decided to try a sport in which he could be more actively involved. He tried out for tennis, made the team, and found himself interested and excited. In short, because Brad knew the mood diagram, he was able to choose an activity that put him in the comfortable middle range of moods and to avoid one that plunged him into the uncomfortable low range.

Helping kids to **identify** the moods they're experiencing always means a healthy growth in self-knowledge. When we also teach them **specific strategies** (like the ones discussed in this chapter) for maintaining their moods in the middle range, we're significantly increasing their chances of not developing problems with alcohol or other drugs. The following list makes additional suggestions.

How to Help Kids Manage Their Moods

Things to Do

- Model healthful eating habits. Avoid junk foods, and plan regular meals that include all the basic food groups.

- Establish routines for bedtime and sleeping time that allow all members of the family to get the sleep they need. Quiet times, after certain hours, are essential for kids of all ages. For example, on school nights kids in grade school might well be expected to be in bed by 8:30 or 9:00; junior high, 9:30 or 10:00; and high school, 10:00 or 10:30, depending on the morning wake-up time.

- Do activities with kids that teach them good exercise habits and at the same time show them that exercise is **fun.** The list is endless: tennis, basketball, skating, walking, jogging, swimming, to mention only a few.

- Help the family to discuss openly the mood levels of individual family members and of the family as a whole. When a family member sinks into boredom or edges toward irritability, for instance, being able to talk about it helps the person to see where he or she is heading and to ward off trouble.

- Become aware of your own moods and be willing to discuss with the kids how those moods affect the kids and others around you. Modeling this willingness will teach kids a lot about maintaining their own moods in the comfortable middle range. Also, it's important to be responsive to kids as they give us feedback about our moods. ("Dad, all week you've been irritable at the dinner table. Is something wrong?" "Oh, really? I honestly didn't know that. I'm glad you mentioned it.")

Things to Avoid

- Instead of having junk food in the house, have on hand a supply of carrot and celery sticks plus other cut-up vegetables, along with natural dips, fruit, and popcorn.

- Help kids avoid confining themselves to passive activities such as watching TV or sitting on the sidelines at all sporting events. Encourage their active participation in sports, hobbies, outside activities. Get involved with them, support their teams, go to their games.

- Direct your kids to have jobs that don't interfere with proper daily habits associated with basic needs such as proper nutrition, sleep, exercise, and relaxation.

Summary

Mood-maintenance is a life skill which, when undeveloped, can lead to alcohol or other drug problems. Young people often resort to using alcohol or other drugs as an attempt to self-medicate moods they find uncomfortable or unpleasant. By teaching our kids specific and healthful ways to maintain their moods in the desirable mid-range, we're significantly reducing their vulnerability to alcohol and other drug use.

10

Communication Skills

Chemical dependence is often called a disease of loneliness. Many young people try to get rid of their loneliness by turning to alcohol or other drugs as a means of building up their confidence so they can meet people and make friends. Satisfying interpersonal relationships, by contrast, reduce a young person's tendency to seek alcohol and other drugs. The U.S. military, for example, has found that young GIs stationed in places where they can have the benefit of such relationships are far less likely to have alcohol and other drug problems than those in isolated posts.

Unfortunately, in our fast-paced and increasingly mobile culture, many young people (as well as adults) feel an increasing sense of isolation and alienation. To combat this we must teach our kids life skills that will help them establish positive relationships with other young people and adults too.

Communication skills are among the most important tools that kids need as a way of connecting with others. As we might expect, and as researchers keep telling us, kids who are good communicators are well accepted by others, so they're well on their way to establishing the personal contacts that prevent loneliness and its predictable effects, among which are alcohol and other drug problems.

Communication skills are equally important to parents as a means of building and maintaining good relationships with their kids.

The Ineffective Communicator

Kids learn their communication habits, good or bad, primarily from parents who model them. When we want to teach our kids communication skills, then, we need to look first at our own communication habits to see which are effective and which are ineffective. It helps to start by inspecting the ineffective ones, because we often unwittingly fall into them. One way to approach them is to ask ourselves honestly if we belong to any of the following categories of ineffective communicators.

- **The Drill Sergeant:** The primary goal of the drill sergeant is to demand submission. The drill sergeant's communication often uses threats, punishment, ridicule, or harsh methods. The drill sergeant often uses language such as "What do you mean, you feel like crying? No son or daughter of mine is going to be a bawl-baby!" or "Being afraid of the water is no excuse for not jumping in. The only way to learn to swim is to jump into water that's over your head and learn how not to drown." The message that kids really get from drill sergeants is that it's not safe to share feelings or show weaknesses in their presence, because they'll be ridiculed or demeaned.

- **The Prosecuting Attorney:** The goal of the prosecuting attorney is to get the facts; nothing else is important. The prosecuting attorney often resorts to cross examination or verbal trickery in an effort to get all the information.

Son: (looking sad and dejected): "I didn't make the basketball team."

Parent: "But why? Didn't you put out for the coach?"

Son: "Yeah, I think I worked hard, but the kid who beat me out was better."

Parent: "You must have done something wrong. What was it? Either you weren't working hard enough or you just didn't care. If you'd have done your best, you'd have made the team."

Son: "You don't understand. You just think I'm a big loser."

The message kids get from the prosecuting attorney is "I don't count; it's not important how I feel."

- **The Egomaniac:** The goal of the egomaniac, even if it's not consciously intended, is to talk about only what he or she is interested in and not to listen at all to the other person. A typical tactic of the egomaniac is switching subjects. No matter what the young person tries to talk about, the conversation always returns to the egomaniac. He or she is incapable of listening to anything that doesn't arouse immediate interest or give gratification to him or her. An egomaniac grandmother wants to talk about nothing except her new grandchild. An avid golfer won't let the conversation turn to anything except his golf game. The egomaniac often uses such tactics as "You think your football coach is tough on you? Well, when I was your age we used to. . ." or "I'm sure glad you made the honor roll. Did I ever tell you about the way I felt when I . . .?"

The message kids get is "What's the use in trying? Whatever I do is never as good as what he (she) did."

- **The Comedian:** The goal of the comedian is to take the focus off uncomfortable topics by making others laugh. For example, if a child has been caught cheating in school, instead of dealing with the child's feelings that prompted the cheating, the comedian will make a joke to cover up the seriousness of the problem. "Well, I'm real happy you haven't murdered anyone yet. Heh, heh." The comedian often uses sarcasm or cynicism couched in humor to get his or her point across. "You sure look like a stuffed monkey in that outfit." It's frustrating when kids try to communicate with the comedian, who can always counter any criticism with "I was just having a little fun" or "Just teasing." "But the method isn't funny, and it does hurt. And ultimately the comedian's approach teaches kids a terrible habit: covering up their true feelings by laughing when they're actually in trouble and hurting inside.

- **The Psychiatrist:** The goal of the psychiatrist is to analyze, diagnose, and then prescribe the appropriate action to solve a youngster's problem. "I think what's really behind these arguments with your sister is that she has developed a very passive-aggressive attitude toward you, and I think you're caught in an attention-getting ploy that will . . ." The psychiatrist might appear to be an effective listener but he or she actually undermines communication by assuming too much responsibility for the child's behavior. This communicates to the child that there will always be someone to give him or her the right answer and that there's no need to learn to think for oneself.

- **The Avoider:** The goal of the avoider is the same as that of the comedian: to sidetrack uncomfortable concerns, no matter how serious they are. Instead of using humor, though, the avoider simply drops any heated or controversial topic. "Well, I certainly agree that nuclear weapons are a problem, but my dad always told me never to argue religion or politics. Did you see what the Yankees did yesterday? Eight runs in the fifth inning!" The message kids get from the avoider is that conflict and controversy are dangerous and should be avoided at all costs, even if it means covering up our feelings or violating our convictions to avoid "a scene."

Here's how each type of ineffective communicator might respond to a 12 year old who says, "I don't have time to clean my room and do my homework, too. You always expect me to be perfect."

- **The Drill Sergeant:** "You march right back upstairs this instant, and don't show your face down here until you've finished both jobs."

- **The Prosecuting Attorney:** "How much homework have you done? And why haven't you done it? If you don't get the grades you promised, there'll be hell to pay around here."

- **The Egomaniac:** "When I was your age I not only had to keep my room clean and do my homework; I had three cows to milk every morning and evening."

- **The Comedian:** "What do you mean, you can't do both at the same time? You seem to do pretty well keeping two or three girls on the hook all at the same time."

- **The Psychiatrist:** "I think your problem is in time management. Let me look at your daily and weekly schedule, and I'll figure out something for you." (As we've pointed out, this supposedly helpful response takes on too much of the youngster's responsibility. It's one thing to be sensitive to our kids' problems; it's another to take them over and solve them. This approach invites either extreme rebellion or extreme compliance.)

- **The Avoider:** "You're probably just tired. Run along and don't worry about it. I'm sure things will be better tomorrow."

These ineffective communication habits can not only destroy good relationships between us and our kids; they can prevent them from ever developing, because we're habitually modeling habits that tend to build walls between us and our kids.

The Effective Communicator

Effective communication primarily involves both speaking and listening. But I've discovered that by far the greatest difficulty in communication between parents and kids is lack of skill in listening. So I'll concentrate on that crucial area. Once we've become aware of any ineffective listening habits, we want to start building up habits that help bond us to our kids. Good listening habits make us available, accessible to our kids. They help us hear not only what our kids are saying but what they're not saying. Effective listeners fall into two categories: the active listener and the facilitative listener.

The Active Listener

The active listener aims at two goals: not only to hear the message being delivered but to reinforce the person delivering the message by giving him or her both verbal and nonverbal feedback. Let's say, for example, that Bill is listening to his son Tom tell about his friend Larry's car accident. Here are some examples of reinforcing the message and giving verbal feedback:

- Appropriate questions: "Where were Larry's parents when the accident happened?" "Was Larry driving the family car, or his own?"

- Clarifying content: "Do you mean Larry didn't even try to slow down, or do you mean he tried to slow down but couldn't?"

- Appropriate verbal encouragement: "Uh huh, I see." "Go on." "Tell me more."

- Good eye contact: looking directly at the person speaking in an open, nonthreatening way.

- A facial expression that indicates interest, understanding, empathy. Being responsive means laughing when things are funny and generally responding nonverbally in an appropriate way.

The Facilitative Listener

The active listener, who listens in such a way as to hear the content and at the same time to reinforce the child giving the message, is most effective when the child just needs a sounding board, an opportunity to ventilate ideas and feelings in a safe environment. Active listening will probably make up 80 to 90 percent of the listening time we spend with our kids. But sometimes our kids need more. They need help in bringing their **underlying feelings** to the surface so they can clarify them. That's where the facilitative listener comes in.

The facilitative listener uses the same skills that the active listener does but goes one step further by observing what's not put into words at all. The facilitative listener picks up **nonverbal clues** by watching for **body language** such as facial expressions (angry, sad), gestures (jiggling the feet, wringing the hands), posture (slumped), kinds of breathing (rapid, heavy exhaling), skin color (flushed, pale), and tone of voice (quiet, anxious). All these can indicate the child's real feelings—feelings that the words themselves don't indicate at all, or that the words might be trying to conceal or even falsify. The observant parent will pick up this body language, interpret what feelings it signifies, and use the clues to help the child clarify his or her feelings.

Son: (looking sad, dejected, posture slumped): "I didn't make the team."

Parent: "It looks as if you have a lot of feelings about that."

Son: "No, it's OK. I'm kind of mad at the coach, but I'll get over it."

Parent: "You look like you might be feeling more hurt or rejected than angry. Do you have mixed feelings?"

Son: "Well, maybe I do have some of those other feelings, but right now it's easier to be mad."

Parent: "I understand. Sometimes it's hard to feel all of our feelings at once. I'd be glad to talk with you about this later when you're more comfortable. Is that OK?"

Son: "Yeah, maybe we could take a walk after dinner."

Facilitative listening isn't easy for some of us. The temptation is either

- to get caught up only in the content of what's being said and consequently to disregard feelings or

- to become so involved in protecting our kids from their feelings that we insulate them from pain by smothering them with consolation and/or pat answers. ("You shouldn't take it so hard. Hey, how about going to a movie and then stopping for pizza?")

The important assumption behind facilitative listening is that our children have the capacity to work through and deal constructively with their own feelings and their own life situations. But when difficult, emotion-laden situations arise and kids are confused about their own feelings and about possible courses of action, we can be there as facilitative listeners—listeners who help them clarify their feelings and decide on sensible ways out of their problems. Kids whose parents aren't there offering such help often turn to the quick fix of alcohol or other drugs.

Still, that doesn't mean we have to be at the beck and call of our kids every moment of the day or night. Ordinarily, let's say, we should be able to listen to the six o'clock news undisturbed. Unless it's clear that there's a real emergency we can gently let our kids know that while we're not available right now, we are interested and concerned about them and their problems and we'll be glad to talk with them just a bit later, at such-and-such a time. But then we have to be sure to get back to them at that time or risk our losing their trust and confidence and their losing their self-worth.

How to Help Kids Communicate

Things to Do

- Become more aware of your listening style. Look at the situations where you fall into ineffective listening (e.g., when you're busy, disturbed by financial or job concerns), and consider ways to listen more effectively.

- Ask others (spouse, kids, coworkers, close friends) for feedback on how well you listen. Check again after working on it for a few weeks, and see if you've improved.

- Gently give your kids feedback on their listening habits. Ask them to give you feedback on your listening habits, too. Work with each other to establish good active and facilitative listening skills.

- Talk with your kids about relationships and the role of communication. Games such as "Telephone" (the simple game of passing a message from one person to the next and comparing the message once it has been heard and repeated by four or five people) and other games demonstrate the importance of good listening habits.

- When you don't have time to listen right now, make sure to get back to your kids within a reasonable amount of time. It's important to acknowledge their problems and to commit yourself to helping.

Things to Avoid

- Don't expect yourself to be a perfect listener all the time.

- Don't expect your kids to be perfect listeners. Like you, they need time to develop their listening habits. Kids by nature are pretty wrapped up in themselves.

Summary

Communication skills are a basic tool in establishing healthy, satisfying relationships. Because kids (and adults) tend to use alcohol or other drugs as a substitute for relationships, our own communication skills and the communication skills we teach our kids are essential in helping them avoid alcohol and other drugs.

Kids learn styles of communication primarily by observing others, especially parents. So the communication styles we model for them are crucially important. By becoming active and facilitative listeners for our kids we're not only making an invaluable contribution to their lives; we're making ourselves better persons and better parents by being more accessible to them.

11

Refusal Skills

Ellen, a seventh grader, was somewhat shy. When Kathy moved into the neighborhood she and Ellen began hanging out together. Ellen liked being around Kathy because Kathy was outgoing, a lot of fun, and instinctively knew how to attract boys.

When Kathy offered to share some vodka with her, Ellen was surprised. Ellen had promised her parents she wouldn't use alcohol or other drugs, and she took the promise seriously, but she really liked Kathy. She also envied how easily Kathy could talk with others, and she wanted to be like her.

When Kathy assured her that a couple of drinks of vodka would make her feel more relaxed and confident, Ellen wanted to say no, but the words just wouldn't form in her mouth. She was caught. Why? Because she was afraid. She lacked refusal skills.

The Meaning and Importance of Refusal Skills

What are refusal skills? Very simply put, they're the skills that enable us to say no when we want to say no, and to do it effectively. Why are they important? Because the story of Ellen and Kathy is being reenacted thousands of times a day, in one form or another, all over our land. Wherever kids go, they're meeting other kids or adults who keep inviting them, even urging them, to use alcohol or other drugs. The way they respond to those invitations and urgings can literally be a matter of life or death for them. And their response depends, in turn, on whether they've learned how to use refusal skills. Both common sense and the best of current research tell us that if we want to prevent our kids from getting involved in alcohol and other drugs, we have to teach them, among other things, how to use refusal skills. This chapter presents the highlights of what parents need to know.

The Continuum of Refusal Styles

There are many ways or styles of saying no. For instance (it's one book among many), see *Your Perfect Right: A Guide to Assertive Living* by Robert E. Alberti and Michael L. Emmons (Available from Impact Publishers, San Luis Obispo, California, 6th ed., 1990). It describes a continuum or steady line of refusal styles that range from passive to aggressive, with the desirable assertive style falling in the middle.

Passive   Assertive   Aggressive

Let's take a look at each of these styles. We'll consider the two extremes only briefly and then focus on the style we really want our kids to learn: the assertive.

The Passive Refusal Style

Persons who use the passive style of refusal tend to say **maybe** a lot more than they say no. They often report feeling obligated to go along with others, or at least to appear to be going along.

A typical passive refusal often sounds something like token resistance followed by compliance: "I'd really rather not, at least not right now. But if everybody else is . . .. well, maybe." The person who uses this style would generally rather not go along with the crowd but lacks the confidence and skills to take a stand.

The Aggressive Refusal Style

Persons who use this refusal style typically overstate their objections and go so far as to be indignant and/or morally outraged at what's been proposed to them. Their indignation or moral outrage might seem at first glance to represent deep convictions about their beliefs and values, but it's usually more of a compensation for insecurity and feelings of self-doubt.

Those who use this aggressive style of refusal often resort to insults or threats, and their whole manner shows that they don't really respect others. A typical aggressive style of refusal sounds like "What? Me drink that stuff? You guys must be a bunch of morons." The reaction of their peers is predictable: They harass and ostracize the offender, who ends up friendless and bitter—and a likely prospect for alcohol or other drug abuse.

The Assertive Refusal Style

This is the refusal style we want to help our kids learn. It avoids the extreme, unproductive behavior of both the passive and the aggressive styles and, unlike them, really is a skill, a truly desirable method of handling the delicate problem of how to say no. (I must remind you that the following remarks on the assertive refusal style are by no means a treatment of the much broader area called assertiveness or assertiveness training. They confine themselves to one aspect of assertiveness, the assertive refusal style, because it bears directly on the whole point of this book: ways in which parents can help kids to say no to alcohol and other drugs.)

Persons who have mastered the assertive refusal style are in a powerful position when they're invited to get involved in alcohol or other drugs. They're able to let it be known firmly, forcefully, clearly but gently that the answer is no. They express themselves confidently, calmly, in a dignified way that shows they've thought over this whole matter and have reached a decision on what's best for them. In other words, they have principles, and they're sticking to them; they respect themselves.

At the same time, though, their answer and their whole manner shows that although they don't want to get involved in alcohol or other drugs, they respect the persons they're talking to. They don't resort to self-righteous indignation, anger, insults, or threats. The end result is that they've maintained their own position but haven't alienated others or isolated themselves. Some examples of this style might be:

- "No, I can't. I want to stay eligible for football."
- "No. I just can't handle that stuff at all."

- "No. I promised my parents I wouldn't."
- "Thanks, but I'm crazy enough without it."
- "No, thanks. I always have a good time without it."

What can parents do to help their kids learn this assertive refusal style? Here are three major recommendations: Help them develop confidence; help them practice assertive refusal skills; reinforce their individuality.

Help Kids Develop Confidence

Confidence is crucial in developing effective refusal skills. Kids who don't feel sure of themselves can't calmly and firmly assert their values and decisions. We can help them develop confidence in a number of ways.

1. **Express your love for them openly and often,** both by words and by body language such as a hug, a pat on the back, an arm around the waist. We tend to assume that kids know we love them, but in childhood years and early adolescence they often feel unloved, unwanted.

2. **Give kids feedback on specific instances of good behavior.** Positive feedback always feels good, but it's especially effective in building up a kid's confidence when we link it directly with something accomplished. Here's how to do it:

   - Describe the behavior. ("Johnny, you did a great job of cleaning your room!")

   - Express your feelings about it. ("I'm really happy to see you putting so much effort into your chores. Good for you!")

   - Encourage more of the same. ("Keep up the good work!")

3. **When confronting kids on negative behavior, make sure they know you're focusing on their behavior, not on them as persons.** If they feel you're criticizing them as persons, they take it to mean you think they're **bad persons,** and this tears down their confidence and self-esteem. When they know you're objecting to their behavior, though, they can still think of themselves as good persons who have made a mistake—a huge difference in self-image.

Here's how to confront negative behavior in a way that will firmly express your displeasure but will positively build up the child's confidence:

- Describe the behavior clearly. ("John, you didn't make your bed today.")

- Express your feelings. ("I'm disappointed.")

- Suggest a redeeming behavior. ("I think you should make your bed before you turn on the TV.")

- Involve yourself in a helpful way. ("I'll show you how to make your bed if you want me to, but I expect you to do it on your own from now on. The next time you don't, you'll lose TV privileges for the evening.")

This carefully controlled kind of confrontation actually builds up kids' confidence. Deep inside (even if they hardly realize it themselves, or even if they explicitly object), they sense that you care enough about them to be concerned about their behavior and to spend time and energy on their problem. Your offer of personal help is especially convincing. Then, too, they've gotten one more lesson in how to behave as budding adults; they know more about how to act properly in society, so they're more confident about asserting themselves successfully with others. A simple example about a minor point of social manners might help make my point. A child might at first think it's of no importance to learn which is the salad fork, but forever after that he or she has no worries about making an embarrassing blunder. The result: greater confidence.

Help Kids Practice Assertive Refusal Skills

Kids develop the capacity to say no at about 18 months. During the terrible twos, "no" seems to be the only word they know. Trying as those early years are for parents, they mark important initial attempts at assertiveness. In grade school, when social pressures develop, youngsters increasingly need to practice refusal skills so they won't weakly go along with the crowd in everything. Here are two ways parents can help:

- Give your kids opportunities to discuss problem situations that often occur, such as saying no to a bully, to an older kid, to a friend who wants him to be his personal errand boy and run to the store and get him a can of soda.

- Practice difficult situations. ("Okay, I'm a bully. I want that jacket of yours, kid." Or "I'm your friend Jimmy. How about smoking a joint together? Your parents don't want you to? What are you, a baby or something? Does the good little boy do everything Mommy and Daddy want?")

These discussions and role-playing sessions answer many needs—among them, learning firsthand the differences between passive, aggressive, and assertive styles of refusal and also letting our kids know that we understand the types of situations they face every day.

Help Kids by Reinforcing Their Individuality

During the pre-teen years, kids are experimenting more and more with what it means to be an individual. While this conduct may be somewhat threatening to parents (the age-old problem of letting go that we discussed early in this book), we should reinforce kids by letting them know—by both words and deeds—that we understand and approve their natural movement toward becoming mature, independent individuals. More specifically:

• We should recognize and discuss with them their unique qualities and abilities. Patti loves to deal with little kids. This unselfishness is wonderful. Might it indicate abilities in the child development field? Nursing? Social work? Mark loves the outdoors and wildlife. In these days of huge environmental problems, his interest can find many satisfying outlets. Might he get into government work to see that the proper laws get passed and enforced? Or be a biologist working directly with wildlife?

• Two skills already covered in this book fit neatly into any discussion of individuality. Feeling-processing skills (Chapter 6) make it clear that these feelings are yours, not someone else's; the better you learn to identify, own, and express them, the more you reveal your unique personality, your individuality. Decision-making skills (Chapter 7) show you that these are your decisions, to be made in light of your personality, your own concrete situation, and that you (not someone else) will be responsible for them.

• Bizarre (to parents) adolescent behavior can be very trying, but it's a way kids use to assert their individuality: showy earrings, outlandish (again, to us) dress and hairdos. Rather than overreacting by laying down tough and rigid rules to suppress this emerging sense of being unique, we should talk with our kids about their motives for such conduct, show them we recognize their need for increased independence, and all the while make it clear that we support their newly emerging sense of self. When kids clearly lack the willingness to discuss the motivation behind their behavior, we may occasionally need to set limits within which their newly emerging individuality must fit. For instance: "It might be your choice about bathing, but going more than three days without a shower is the limit." Or the other extreme: "I know you want to look nice, but no more than two showers a day." Or "I know that green mohawk haircuts are considered 'in.' I also know it's important for you to have the freedom to express yourself. But you need to consider what impact your individual expression might have on the rest of us."

How to Help Kids Develop Refusal Skills

(Note: Because of the nature of this chapter, some of the following suggestions have already been discussed. We repeat them here in brief form for emphasis and for easier review of the whole group.)

Things to Do

- Express your feelings for your kids openly and often.

- Give them positive feedback in connection with specific instances of good behavior.

- When confronting their negative behavior, make it clear that you're focusing on their behavior, not on them as bad persons.

- Set aside times to discuss how to use refusal skills and to role play situations in which they use those skills.

- Model effective refusal skills by searching out your own possible tendencies toward passive or aggressive refusal styles, and honestly work at getting rid of them.

- Reinforce their emerging sense of individuality.

Things to Avoid

- Don't withhold praise for positive behavior.

- Don't make confrontation a personal attack.

- Don't ridicule or tease your kids about their efforts at being individuals.

Summary

Refusal skills are essential if our kids are to develop the ability to say no to alcohol and other drugs. Simply teaching kids to rehearse pat answers isn't enough. Ineffective refusal styles usually tend to be either overly passive or overly aggressive. The effective refusal style, the assertive, asserts the individual's choice firmly but with respect for others. Parents must help kids learn assertive styles of refusal long before the kids encounter pressures to use alcohol and other drugs.

Part 3 will address additional concerns that, while important, haven't yet been treated in this book. Since kids learn much of what they know about alcohol and other drugs by imitating their parents, Part 3 addresses certain critical issues related to parental alcohol or other drug use as well as special problems faced by parents recovering from alcoholism.

PART 3

Special Issues and Concerns

Introduction

Part 3 will focus on some special issues and concerns, not addressed up to this point, that are nevertheless critical to parenting for prevention.

As I repeatedly pointed out in Parts 1 and 2, modeling is an important parenting technique for helping kids develop the basic life skills that enable them to say no to alcohol and other drugs. That parental duty and challenge of modeling raises some further questions. Do I have to abstain from alcohol to prevent my kids from using it? When does my use of alcohol become excessive, and how does excessive use affect my kids? What about my occasional use of marijuana or other illegal drugs? Also, should I be concerned about my use of drugs that have been prescribed by my physician? My spouse is an alcoholic. How does parental alcoholism affect our kids? Chapter 12 addresses those problems.

Chapter 13 addresses special questions related to the recovering parent. Research indicates that children with alcoholic parents are more likely to develop alcohol or other drug abuse problems. This chapter recommends some specific action the recovering parent can take to minimize the impact of parental alcoholism on these kids.

12

Parental Use of Alcohol and Other Drugs

B ob and Janet are 39 years old. Bob comes from a family of heavy drinkers; Janet's family never drank at all. Bob likes to unwind every evening with two or three beers as he watches TV. Janet has never approved, but Bob's drinking apparently hasn't caused any problems, so she says nothing about it. But when Danny, their 14-year-old, is arrested for possession of marijuana, he argues that using marijuana is really no different from Dad's use of alcohol. The parents are surprised and disturbed by his argument. Could Danny be right?

Excessive Alcohol or Other Drug Use by Parents

This little story raises more questions than whether Danny's using marijuana is really no different from his dad's using alcohol (a question we'll take up a bit later). For instance: is his dad's regular use of alcohol moderate or excessive? Is there anything at all wrong with it? In view of parents' duty of modeling proper behavior for their kids, must parents abstain totally from alcohol or other drugs? Or, to put it somewhat differently, is **any** use of alcohol or other drugs by parents to be considered excessive? Let's talk first about what constitutes excessive use, and why.

Excessive Regular Use

Professionals usually distinguish three kinds of excessive use: regular excessive use, recreational excessive use, symptomatic excessive use. The way Danny's dad uses alcohol really falls into the first category, excessive regular use. That's not to say he's an alcoholic or that he should go into treatment right now. But there's danger in the air. Experts in the field would probably say that he's in late Phase II* of chemical use, where he is regularly seeking the mood swing that alcohol brings. While he may still think of himself as a social drinker, over time his drinking may begin to exact an emotional cost: guilt or shame due to an ever-increasing number of embarrassing incidents related to his use of alcohol. For example, during a night of excessive drinking he makes obscene remarks to one of his daughter's friends who has come to the house to pick her up. If episodes like this continue to happen, he is likely to pass into Phase III of chemical use: harmful dependence. He will have crossed the line between social use and alcoholism. At this point the red light isn't on for Bob, but the amber light is certainly flashing. Later in this chapter we'll discuss the impact of parental alcoholism on kids.

However, the question of whether Bob is an alcoholic or close to being one isn't the only question here. Bob, after all, is

---

*To find out more about how alcohol and other drug use develops, read *Intervention: How to Help Someone Who Doesn't Want Help* by Vernon E. Johnson, D.D. (Minneapolis: The Johnson Institute, 1986).

a **parent,** and as we've repeatedly pointed out, parents are supposed to model the kind of behavior they want their children to emulate. In this important area of alcohol or other drug use, what is Bob modeling? He's telling Danny, by his actions, that having a few beers every night is a perfectly normal, harmless, and effective way of unwinding at the end of a hard day; that it's the way adults do it, and no questions asked. Since this is Danny's real-life introduction to the whole area of alcohol and other drugs, it's no wonder he sees no difference between his use of marijuana and his father's use of alcohol—a dangerous introduction indeed.

Recreational Excessive Use

Parents who habitually overindulge at weddings, family reunions, ball games, and other get-togethers exemplify this type of excessive use. The message they send to their kids is that the way to loosen up, celebrate events, or have fun is to get smashed; that you can't really have fun without alcohol.

Self-medicating Use

When professionals speak of "self-medicating" use in connection with alcohol or other drugs, they're referring to use that's intended to medicate symptoms connected with a specific problem. For instance, those who are exhausted, grieving a loss, depressed, lonely, fearful, or who are nervous about heavy work loads often turn to alcohol or other drugs to get relief from that particular problem.

When those people are parents, they're modeling the wrong double-barreled message to their kids: that this is a perfectly normal, adult way of dealing with difficulties, and that it works—it's a true solution. This message contradicts, however, the sound parenting messages we've been trying to send our kids: that the way to handle life's problems is to develop basic life skills that enable us to process our feelings, maintain our moods in the productive middle zone, and make decisions wisely.

Parents and Total Abstinence

Must parents abstain totally from alcohol to avoid giving kids mixed messages about using it? Not necessarily. I'd like to make three points about this problem: one based on common sense, one based on a simple distinction, and one based on my own experience as a counselor.

1. **Common Sense:** I sometimes hear an argument that, if put into words, would sound something like "If drinking isn't okay for kids, why should it be okay for parents?" Well, lots of things that are okay for adults aren't okay for kids. Adults are supposedly mature and grown-up, and so they have both responsibilities and privileges that kids don't. Adults have the responsibility of making major decisions as a matter of course: about which marriage partner to choose, which career to follow—one that will enable them to provide their own and their family's food, shelter, clothing; about which city and state and even country to live in; about transportation, medical care, and education; about investing thousands or even millions of dollars in homes or businesses; about whether to resist a tyrant even at the risk of torture or death. Since adults are responsible for such heavy choices, they have to be free, basically, to make them.

Kids have no such major responsibilities, ordinarily, and we shouldn't push such huge decisions onto them or even **allow** them to take them on. Kids, especially younger ones, just aren't ready. That's why we don't think it unfair that a 10 year old can't get a driver's license, sign a contract to buy a home, vote, or enter the military. I've found that most kids understand very well that they're not ready for certain decisions and privileges until they reach a certain age and a certain stage of maturity.

As adults we must reserve the right and assume the responsibility to protect children from certain high-risk, potentially dangerous options. Our culture supports us by establishing age limits on most of these activities. We as adults must reinforce those laws not only by setting limits with our kids, but by explaining the wisdom behind them.

When it comes to deciding whether or how to use alcohol or other drugs, adults must face that major decision the way they face other major decisions: freely, but taking full responsibility for their choice. Some of us will make the wrong decision; but some of us will also make the wrong decisions about careers and marriage partners and investments. Privileges and responsibility are the double-edged sword that adults have to carry around every day.

2. **A Simple Distinction:** A rather simple distinction also helps us answer whether adults have to be total abstainers: **Abuse doesn't rule out use.** Automobiles kill thousands of people every year, but we don't banish them from the Earth; we try to get people to drive them responsibly. And so with alcohol. For all the misery that often comes with it,

it's still abuse, not use, that causes the misery. For some people, of course, any use of alcohol turns out to be an abuse; but that's a special case, to be decided in terms of each individual. The same problem hits those exceptional individuals who are allergic to wheat or macadamia nuts: Any use is too much.

3. **Experience:** To me, the most convincing argument against forcing total abstinence on all parents is my own experience and that of my colleagues who have researched the subject thoroughly. What that experience shows clearly is that kids raised in families where adults use alcohol appropriately and in moderate amounts show no stronger or more numerous signs of using alcohol or other drugs than do kids raised in families where parents are total abstainers. Experience teaches that trying to force all people to stop using alcohol (Prohibition) doesn't work. The law will never override the public conscience. Moreover, alcohol isn't destructive in itself—it's the irresponsible use of it and the resulting problems that are.

Parents and Prescription Drugs

In an age when the word "drugs" almost automatically brings to mind illegal drugs such as marijuana or cocaine or heroin, we need to remind ourselves that prescription drugs are indeed drugs and that they can cause problems of serious side effects, abuse, and even addiction. Here are some recommendations about their use.

• Use only drugs prescribed for you by a careful, competent physician, and follow the directions.

- Don't assume that all physicians are aware that drugs they prescribe might have potential for abuse and/or chemical dependence. In practice, some physicians overlook that danger.

- Get a second physician's opinion if you have reason to doubt whether a certain drug is suitable for you.

- Always inform a physician about any drugs prescribed for you by another physician; there may be a danger of over-medication or of incompatible drugs.

- Check other sound sources of information about drugs: pharmacists (most of whom are very knowledgeable), well-recommended books that list and evaluate drugs; experienced nurses; sensible friends whose experience with a given drug may well be invaluable as a firsthand report.

- Never mix prescription drugs with alcohol.

In this area of prescription drugs, as in so many other areas, our **modeling** of proper use is the strongest message we can send our kids about what's appropriate for them.

Parents and Illegal Drugs

I've worked with many parents who grew up in the sixties and seventies when marijuana was so popular its use was widely taken for granted. Some of those parents still feel justified in using marijuana occasionally, arguing that it's no different from using alcohol.

When parents use marijuana, though, the message they send their kids is different from the one they send when they use alcohol moderately. Despite the fact that both are mind-altering drugs, marijuana adds a new, undesirable message. For the hard fact is that marijuana is illegal. So when parents use it—or any other illegal drug—they tell their kids, "We're above the law." Kids easily arrive at a more general conclusion: that limits, rules, and laws are for **others**. "Mom and Dad do what they want and when they want to. Why can't I?"

Parents and Secret Use of Illegal Drugs

Some parents counter the previous objection to illegal drugs with "Yes, I see what you mean. But we just don't tell our kids we're using illegal drugs. So there's no harm done." When I hear that, I'm tempted to say, "You must be kidding." But I try to be polite; I remind them that it's impossible to keep such secrets from kids, who are sizing us up all the time and who have seemingly limitless resources for uncovering our secrets. When they uncover this one, we've modeled not only lawbreaking, but hypocrisy as well. Hardly a prescription for effective parenting!

Effects of Parental Addiction on Kids

Addiction to any form of mind-altering drugs in parents has terribly destructive effects on kids, both physically and psychologically. Here are some of them in very brief form.

Physical Effects*

- **FAS—Fetal Alcohol Syndrome:** One of the three most frequent causes of birth defects associated with mental retardation that occurs as a direct result of a mother's alcohol abuse or addiction.

- **FAE—Fetal Alcohol Effects:** More common birth defects such as low birth weight that can produce developmental damage to the child—e.g., learning disabilities also associated with mother's use or abuse of alcohol.

Psychological Effects

In Margaret Cork's early but classic study on children of alcoholics, *The Forgotten Children,*** the author reports these statistics on children of alcoholic parents:

- 98% feel that relationships within the family are affected.

- 97% feel that relationships outside the family are affected.

- 94% feel unsure of themselves, lack confidence.

- 97% feel unwanted by one or both parents.

- 77% feel constantly ashamed or hurt and get upset and cry easily.

---

*Taken from *Alcohol/Drug Dependent Women: New Insights Into Their Special Problems, Treatment, Recovery* by Sheila B. Blume, M.D. (Minneapolis: The Johnson Institute, 1988).

***The Forgotten Children: A Study of Children with Alcoholic Parents* by R. Margaret Cork (Toronto: Alcoholism and Drug Addiction Research Foundation, 1969).

In brief, the impact of parental addiction on children is devastating. Not only do addicted parents model inappropriate use of alcohol and other drugs, but they fail to build a home environment that gives kids the pervasive sense of security they need if they're ever to develop the basic life skills. Instead of developing those positive, healthy life skills that help the emerging adult to exercise and strengthen his or her wings, gradually become an independent adult, and in due time move out of the family circle and use those skills confidently in the outside world, the child in an alcoholic home develops **survival skills**—skills that help him or her merely to survive in that abnormal alcoholic environment. Those skills are quite the opposite of the liberating life skills; instead, they become a ball and chain that often keeps the young person tethered, emotionally and/or physically, to the family of origin.*

The family itself begins to center its whole life around the addict—creating a dysfunctional system in which each member functions to protect the user and keep the problem hidden from others. The young person finds himself or herself trapped in relationships that revolve around surviving alcohol or other drug dependence.

How the Non-using Parent Can Help the Kids

Although life in a family where one parent is addicted to alcohol or other drugs often is bleak and seems beyond all help, the non-using parent can do many things to help the children. Here are some of them.

---

* To learn more about what it's like to be raised by alcoholic parents, read *Different Like Me* by Evelyn Leite and Pamela Espeland (Minneapolis: The Johnson Institute, 1987).

- Openly acknowledge your spouse's problem. The most insidious family reaction to addiction is to keep the problem a secret. Kids learn the following rules: Don't talk; don't trust; don't feel. Kids must learn to trust their own perceptions of reality and must be encouraged to act according to them. By acknowledging the existence and devastating effects of addiction, the non-using parent breaks the no-talk rule and frees the children from their isolation so they can find ways to get their own needs met.

- Get help for yourself. Help is always available, whether it's professional or self-help. A good first step is Al-Anon. Al-Anon is a self-help, 12-step program that is free for anyone seeking assistance in solving problems associated with living with an alcoholic or other drug-dependent person. Your reaching out to others will help your kids in at least two ways: You'll be more sane and consequently better able to respond to their needs, and you'll be modeling a constructive life skill that can help your kids learn to begin trusting others and to break the no-talk rule.

- Find a support group for your kids—a group in which kids can talk with peers about their feelings and concerns. Alateen, Alatot, and various other groups for kids with addicted parents, such as Children Are People, are becoming increasingly available. No matter what the kids' ages, they need the opportunity to process their feelings and to relate to others who are experiencing troubles similar to their own. Such contacts help kids overcome their own feelings of isolation and uniqueness—the feeling that they're drifting, helpless and alone on an endless, menacing ocean.

Summary

Clearly, the choices we make regarding alcohol and other drugs will affect the decisions our kids will inevitably make about them. How we model appropriate use is therefore critical.

Despite our best attempts, it's naive to think we can keep our use a secret from our kids—a secret that includes what we use, how much we use, when and even where we use. They'll know.

Parental addiction does further damage to kids because it disables the family in ways that encourage kids to develop survival skills rather than true, positive life skills. Unfortunately, survival skills often don't transfer into school or work as effectively as the life skills these kids are lacking. Parental addiction also sets kids up to carry that dysfunctional survivor mode of living into adulthood and to pass it on to their own kids eventually.

In the next chapter we'll look at the special challenges facing the addicted parent who is involved in a recovery program and wants both to minimize the damage caused by his or her alcohol or other drug problem and to maximize the positive effects of sobriety.

13

The Recovering Parent

Dave has been sober for four years. He went to treatment when Eddie, an only child, was eight years old.

Eddie wasn't involved in his dad's treatment; everyone thought he was too young at the time. But he vividly remembers his dad's drinking, especially the last year: endless family arguments, his dad coming home drunk and shouting obscenities at the neighbors, the police coming again and again after the neighbors' complaints, and finally his dad leaving, suitcase in hand, for the hospital.

Yet it seemed that Eddie was never really affected by that whole experience. He did well in school, seemed happy enough, and really helped out Mom while Dad was gone.

Now that Eddie is 12, though, he's like a different person: withdrawn, isolated, and hanging out with a crowd of kids known for using alcohol and other drugs. Dave blames himself. He feels that his alcoholism has created a barrier between himself and his son that keeps him from being available as a parent at this crucial time in Eddie's life. When he and Eddie try to talk, Dave always ends up angry, and Eddie stares at the wall in silence.

I've seen this scenario repeated many times as recovering parents are confronted with the dysfunctional behavior some of their kids develop even though the parent is now sober.

Addiction creates open wounds in all of those directly affected by the addict. Until recently, however, professionals in the field of addiction, as well as parents themselves, have frequently ignored the wounds carried by children in alcoholic families, especially by younger children—probably because younger children do a good job of seeming to be unaffected by the addiction. We've also avoided looking at their wounds because when we do, the depth of their pain can be frightening.

Since many children of alcoholics have been so neglected, the bulk of this chapter on the recovering parent is really devoted to them: first, to help parents understand what usually happens to kids when a parent quits using and gets on the road to recovery; and second, to focus on three major areas in which the recovering parent can help heal kids' wounds. The final section of the chapter offers some other suggestions to the recovering parent.

What Happens to Kids
When a Parent Quits Drinking

When a parent stops drinking and begins recovery, what happens to the children can usually be summed up in three steps.

Step I: Putting Band-Aids on Deep Wounds

Usually no attention is paid to the pain and suffering of the children until a parent quits drinking. Possibly kids will participate in only one group session or perhaps in an education program at the center where the parent is in treatment. The children's immediate bleeding may be stopped and Band-Aids applied to their wounds, but the primary focus stays on the recovery process of the addicted parent. Providing treatment for the children is often given only cursory attention. This leaves the young person only one choice: to ignore the pain and the impact of the parent's addiction and pretend nothing is going on. This is usually fairly easy for the children, since they've been taught over and over "Don't talk; don't trust; don't feel." As the child ignores the pain, eventually the bleeding stops and the wounds form hardened scabs.

Step II: The Scabbing Over of Wounds

As the parent continues to participate in a recovery program, the deeper wounds of the children often go unnoticed. As others often fail to acknowledge those wounds, kids develop defense mechanisms to cope with the feelings they've experienced and continue to carry as the result of the painful events that happened during the drinking years. For example, they pretend that the feelings from being ignored, yelled at, and sometimes beaten by Dad don't even exist. Feelings of hurt and anger often fester and turn into deep-seated resentment. Feelings of being different, isolated, and unwanted create a sense of shame.

Even though scabs form over the wounds, children often continue to carry unresolved feelings centered around that resentment and shame. Those feelings undermine not only the relationship between the recovering parent and the children, but also the children's sense of self-confidence.

Step III: The Eruption

Usually those unresolved feelings erupt during early adolescence (often ages 11-14), because at this stage kids tend to act out their feelings. Outward displays of hostility, anger, and rage are common, as are feelings of self-doubt, confusion, and self-hatred. As those feelings erupt, the recovering parent and the children typically become pitted against each other as they dump their unresolved pain on each other.

Parent: "You don't care about me at all. I was up till 2 o'clock in the morning waiting for you to come home from that party."

Son: "What do you mean, I don't care? When you were drinking, you were never home, and you never came to one of my games. I'll always hate you for that."

Not only has the child of the alcoholic carried unresolved pain, but the recovering parent often has had little opportunity to verbalize any of the depth of the guilt he or she has felt toward the child. With time that guilt often turns inward to self-hatred and anger. When, after years of being ignored, these festering feelings are first lanced (often in the course of the parent's treatment for alcoholism), it's not unusual or surprising that there's an emotional outpouring of feelings springing from vague, unfocused anger. But under the anger lie feelings of guilt, shame, and humiliation that need to be resolved.

At this point children can very easily develop a serious problem with alcohol or other drugs. These children are more likely to experiment with alcohol or other drugs at an earlier age than their friends do; worse, their experimentation will often develop into a problem far more quickly. Why? Professionals give various explanations:

- These children are at high risk to develop alcohol or other drug problems because of the strong possibility of a genetic predisposition to alcoholism.

- The parent has modeled alcohol or other drug use as a way to cope with pain and stress.

- Erupting pain is so powerful that mind-altering chemicals are extremely attractive and effective in covering up the pain.

How to Help Kids Recover

The pain that parental alcoholism causes kids is predictably devastating, but the recovering parent can help in at least three major ways.

Help Kids to Face the Pain

It can be very difficult for a parent just to see the deep-seated resentment, rage, and shame that his or her addiction has brought upon the children. For example, a teenage boy who was seldom disciplined by his father, but who now sees his dad attempting to assume a parental role he had abdicated in favor of alcohol will often vehemently reject these attempts. It can be more difficult yet to help such a parent face his or her own pain. But it can be done.

The ability of a recovering parent to be helpful to his or her child in pain as a result of parental neglect or mistreatment will depend on some basic attitudes in that parent: willingness to help, courage, patience. But it depends, too, on using and teaching a major life skill we discussed in Chapter 6: the ability to process feelings. (Reviewing that chapter might help to refresh your memory.) Essentially, you will recall, the skill consists of identifying one's feelings, owning them (accepting them as one's own), and expressing them. It would be hard to imagine a situation in which that life skill could be more valuable than when a recovering parent sits down with his or her own kids to help them face and resolve their own painful feelings. The parent can signal in many ways that those feelings are understandable and normal and that he or she is willing to help the children know about them and work through them.

Those feelings won't be processed in one easy session. It will be done the way we peel an onion—one layer after another.

Son: "Why do you think you have the right to tell me what to do after all you've put this family through?"

Dad: "I'm only trying to help, to do my part. I'm not trying to run your life. I'm just trying to be your dad."

Son: "It's too late for that. I don't need you! I've learned to take care of myself. Sometimes I wish you didn't quit drinking—you think you're so perfect."

Dad: "I know the pain is still there—I feel it too. You can't begin to know the hours of sleepless nights I've had wondering if I could ever make it up to you and the family. Let's agree to work through these feelings together. I'm willing to try. Are you?"

Son: "I don't know; I need to think about it. I don't want to get hurt again."

Dad: "I understand. Let's talk tomorrow after you've given it some thought."

Help Kids to Reconstruct the Past

It's common for kids to have clouded memories, sometimes no memory at all, of the using episodes that occurred while they lived with an addicted parent. Despite their apparent lack of memory, it's usually important for kids to reconstruct their past in some way.

An exercise I've used with many kids from alcoholic families is to have them bring a journal or notebook and to separate the pages into years. (Usually I suggest going by grades, since kids tend to associate memories with the school calendar, school events, and teachers.) I recommend that each night before going to bed, they spend 10 to 15 minutes relaxing and letting any memory from the family come to mind. When it does, they're to jot down words, sentences, or sketches that describe it. If this exercise is to succeed, parents need to take a real interest in it. They should ask how the journal is going and set aside time each week to discuss memories from the journal as the child is willing to share them.

As kids talk through those events, they'll begin to make sense of their history: where they've been and why things have happened to them. Much of the confusion experienced by children of alcoholic families appears to be caused by a genuine lack of understanding of how the events of their life have fitted together. This isn't surprising when we consider that so much of the life of the addict is steeped in secrecy, unpredictability, chaos, and an unwillingness to acknowledge problems with alcohol and other drugs.

Cooperate in Reestablishing Family Boundaries

In effective families there are clearly defined, healthy, accepted boundaries between parents and children. As I pointed out in another connection, parents make major decisions about where the family lives, how it spends its money, how the house is managed, how the children behave and acquire an education. Kids have a right to be loved and respected, to have all their basic physical and psychological needs taken care of. At the same time, they're expected to cooperate in family life by obeying their parents in all reasonable matters, getting along with their brothers and sisters, and performing tasks suitable to their condition, such as keeping their room in good order, doing some household chores, and running errands.

As addiction to alcohol or other drugs takes over in a family, though, those boundaries begin to break down. I've worked with families where kids in effect became parents and parents became kids. A 10-year-old girl might be doing major housecleaning day after day and her 12-year-old brother might be preparing all the meals. A 14-year-old boy might be doing all the grocery shopping and paying the family bills, and his 16-year-old brother might be Mom's confidante who listens to all her troubles, comforts her as best he can, and in effect practically becomes a substitute parent or spouse.

The recovering alcoholic parent must cooperate with both spouse and children to turn that topsy-turvy world right side up. Parents must once again act like parents, kids like kids. In short, roles must be reassigned and really accepted. Parents must be nurturers, leaders, make major family decisions. Kids mustn't be turned into miniature adults. They need time to relax, to play, to be free of making major family decisions, to grow at a natural pace. They need to be given tasks appropriate to their age and stage of development. Above all, they need love, support, encouragement, praise, acknowledgment, and acceptance.

Accomplishing all this turnabout is a task for the whole family, and the recovering alcoholic must be an integral part of it.

Getting Help

Most families recovering from alcoholism need outside help. For some, the support of self-help groups such as Al-Anon and Alateen is enough. Those with a longtime and complex history of alcoholism will need professional help from well-qualified counselors or therapists in going through the major steps in recovery that we've just discussed: facing the pain, reconstructing the past, reestablishing family boundaries.

Here's a suggestion about selecting a therapist or professional counselor. Be sure that the therapist/counselor has a good background not only in the field of chemical dependence, but also in family systems and in the developmental needs of children. Recovery of an alcohol or other drug dependent parent usually means recovery of the whole family, because the **whole family** has been swept into a difficult, traumatic life-style.

Suggestions for the Recovering Parent

- Be willing to talk about the past when kids have questions. It may be very helpful for you to share with them why it's important to you, too, to resolve issues from the past. It can be tempting to avoid this area, but kids really need to sort out their past, and so does the parent. Questions about the past will often come years after the parent has begun sobriety.

- Go slow. Your alcohol or other drug dependence has severely undermined your position as a parent. Don't expect yourself or your kids immediately to feel comfortable with or accepting of this "new" parent.

- Talk about the guilt that you, like every alcohol- or other drug-dependent parent, have eventually felt about not having been there for your kids. Guilt feelings are powerful, but unfortunately are often ignored. To reestablish yourself as a parent, you must acknowledge these feelings and work your way through them.

- Be careful about projecting your own personal situation onto your kids. The typical recovering alcoholic parent is tempted to overreact when kids—especially kids entering adolescence—seem to be on the verge of making the very same mistakes he or she has made. The first impulse is to overreact because of guilty feelings and become overly vigilant and protective. To assume that your kids are exactly like you and therefore will fall into exactly the same traps that you fell into is a mistake. What you can do, instead, is to respond to the kids' **real**—not imagined—needs. That means you need to listen well to what they're **really** saying, observe what they're **really** doing, size up their situation objectively. **Then** you're in a position to offer help.

- Be patient. Recovery is a process that unfolds as you confront sobriety one day at a time. Reestablishing relationships with your kids is also a long, slow process. Sometimes the kids are well into their twenties before they're able to resolve their feelings about an alcoholic parent. Only then can they begin to realize that parents are people, too—not gods or goddesses, but imperfect human beings like themselves—who've proved it by making lots of mistakes and yet are willing to work through them.

Afterword

In the past 30 years, many approaches to preventing kids from getting involved with alcohol and other drugs have been tried, but with minimal results. What most of these approaches have had in common is that they've been focused outside the family. Yet the best research has made two points increasingly clear. First, prevention efforts must be reinforced **in the home.** Second, what kids need most is a set of **positive, practical life skills** that will give them the tools for facing all of life's pressures and stress without resorting to alcohol or other drugs.

In this book I've brought those two important points together. First, I've directed it to parents. Second, since my long experience as a counselor has convinced me that parents are both eager and perfectly willing to teach their kids those life skills they need, I've written this book to show them how to do it.

Resources

The following groups and organizations can provide additional information on prevention of alcohol and other drug use by children and adolescents.

Addiction Research Foundation
33 Russell Street
Toronto, Ontario M5S 2S1
Canada
(416) 595-6056

Al-Anon Family Group Headquarters
1372 Broadway
New York, NY 10018-0862
(212) 302-7240

Alateen
1372 Broadway
New York, NY 10018-0862
(212) 302-7240

A.A.
Alcoholics Anonymous
General Service Office
PO Box 459
Grand Central Station
New York, NY 10163
(212) 686-1100

American Council for Drug Education
204 Monroe Street
Rockville, MD 20850
(301) 294-0600

COAF
Children of Alcoholics
Foundation, Inc.
200 Park Avenue, 31st Floor
New York, NY 10166
(212) 351-2680

Families Anonymous
World Service Office
PO Box 528
Van Nuys, CA 91408
(818) 989-7841

Johnson Institute
7205 Ohms Lane
Minneapolis, MN 55439
1-800-231-5165

Just Say No International
2101 Webster Street
Suite 1300
Oakland, CA 94612
(510) 451-6666;
1-800-258-2766

NCADD
National Council on
Alcoholism and Drug
Dependence
12 West 21st Street
New York, NY 10010
(212) 206-6770

NCADI
National Clearinghouse for
Alcohol/Drug Information
P.O. Box 2345
Rockvllle, MD 20852
(301) 468-2600

*National Federation of
Parents for Drug-Free Youth*
8730 Georgia Avenue
Suite 200
Silver Spring, MD 20910
(301) 585-5437

NIAAA
National Institute on Alcohol
Abuse and Alcoholism
6000 Executive Blvd.
Bethesda, MD 20892-7003
(301) 443-3885

NIDA
National Institute on Drug
Abuse
Room 10-05
Parklawn Building
5600 Fishers Lane
Rockville, MD 20857
(301) 443-6480

PRIDE
National Parents Resource
Institute on Drug Education
10 Park Place South
Suite 540
Atlanta, GA 30303
(404) 577-4500

SADD
Students Against Drunk
Driving
PO Box 800
277 Main Street
Marlboro, MA 01752
1-800-521-SADD

NCA
National Council on
Alcoholism and Drug
Dependence Hopeline
12 West 21st Street, 7th Floor
New York NY 10010
1-800-NCA-CALL

Narcotics Anonymous
World Services Office, Inc.
PO Box 9999
Van Nuys, CA 91409
(818) 780-3951

NACOA
National Association for
Children of Alcoholics, Inc.
11426 Rockville Pike
Suite 100
Rockville, MD 20852
(301) 468-0985

IBCA
Institute on Black Chemical
Abuse
2614 Nicollet Avenue South
Minneapolis, MN 55408
(612) 871-7878

Index

JOHNSON INSTITUTE®

When the Johnson Institute first opened its doors in 1966, few people knew or believed that alcoholism was a disease. Fewer still thought that anything could be done to help the chemically dependent person other than to wait for him or her to "hit bottom" and then pick up the pieces.

We've spent over twenty-five years spreading the good news that chemical dependence is a *treatable* disease. Through our publications, films, videos, audiocassettes, and our training and consultation services, we've given hope and help to hundreds of thousands of people across the country and around the world. The intervention and treatment methods we've pioneered have restored shattered careers, healed relationships with coworkers and friends, saved lives, and brought families back together.

Today the Johnson Institute is an internationally recognized leader in the field of chemical dependence prevention, intervention, treatment, and recovery. Individuals, organizations, and businesses, large and small, rely on us to provide them with the tools they need. Schools, universities, hospitals, treatment centers, and other health care agencies look to us for experience, expertise, innovation, and results. With care, compassion, and commitment, we will continue to reach out to chemically dependent persons, their families, and the professionals who serve them.

Johnson Institute
7205 Ohms Lane
Minneapolis, Minnesota 55439-2159
United States or Canada: 800-231-5165

Order Form

Need a copy for a friend? You can order directly from:

Johnson Institute
7205 Ohms Lane
Minneapolis, MN 55439
(612) 831-1630

For faster service, call TOLL-FREE: **1-800-231-5165**
Or fax your order to: **1-612-831-1631**
Be sure to ask for a free catalog!

Parenting for Prevention
**How to Raise a Child to Say No to Alcohol and Other Drugs
For Parents, Teachers, and Other Concerned Adults**

Revised Edition

by David J. Wilmes

ORDER #P071   NUMBER OF COPIES _____   x $12.95 _____

SHIPPING: ONE BOOK $2.50

ADDITIONAL COPIES _____   x $1.00 _____

TOTAL ORDER _____

Payment enclosed: ☐ Check   ☐ Money Order

Bill my credit card: ☐ AMERICAN EXPRESS   ☐ DISCOVER   ☐ MasterCard   ☐ VISA

Account Number: _____

Expiration Date: _____

Signature on Card: _____

SHIPPING ADDRESS

Name (please print) _____

Address _____

City _____ *State* _____ *Zip* _____

Telephone (_____) _____

Order Form

Need a copy for a friend? You can order directly from:

Johnson Institute
7205 Ohms Lane
Minneapolis, MN 55439
(612) 831-1630

For faster service, call TOLL-FREE: **1-800-231-5165**
Or fax your order to: **1-612-831-1631**
Be sure to ask for a free catalog!

Parenting for Prevention
How to Raise a Child to Say No to Alcohol and Other Drugs
For Parents, Teachers, and Other Concerned Adults

Revised Edition

by David J. Wilmes

ORDER #P071   NUMBER OF COPIES _____ x $12.95 _____

SHIPPING: ONE BOOK $2.50

ADDITIONAL COPIES _____   x $1.00 _____

TOTAL ORDER _____

Payment enclosed: ☐ Check   ☐ Money Order

Bill my credit card: ☐ AMERICAN EXPRESS   ☐ DISCOVER   ☐ MasterCard   ☐ VISA

Account Number: _____

Expiration Date: _____

Signature on Card:_____

SHIPPING ADDRESS

Name (please print) _____

Address _____

City _____ *State* _____ *Zip* _____

Telephone (_____) _____